"In this era where DNA tests are surprising so many people with new genetic spins on their origin stories, Patti Eddington's gripping story of filial identity found, lost, then found again is compelling reading, even for those of us who foolishly think we know the intimate details of our beginnings. Beautiful, heart-wrenching and ultimately life-affirming."
 —Michael Zadoorian, author of *The Leisure Seeker*

"Part love letter to her adoptive parents, part origin story with the pacing of a whodunit, *The Girl with Three Birthdays* is full of wry humor and vivid details of small town Michigan girlhood. I was rooting for Patti and her family all the way."
 —Amy Rigby, author of *Girl to City: A Memoir*

"A penetrating account of adoption, tightly-held secrets, and the power of love, told with dogged honesty and heart."
 —Laura Whitfield, author of *Untethered: Faith, Failure, and Finding Solid Ground*

"With enchanting details, luminous coloring, and a masterful balance of fact, humor and lush writing, Patti Eddington lures readers into her indelible story and hugs them tight, sharing her most vulnerable self. A nimble, courageous, and entrancing memoir."
 —Chad V. Broughman, author of *The Fall of Bellwether*

"A beautifully told story of self-discovery with so many twists and turns, I couldn't put it down until I finished it."
—Lisa Cheek, author of *Sit, Cinderella, Sit*

"A riveting memoir . . . Engaging, entertaining, and openhearted, *The Girl with Three Birthdays* is a transformational story of family that will linger in your heart long after you finish the last page.
—Jennifer Cramer-Miller, author of *Incurable Optimist: Living with Illness and Chronic Hope*

THE
GIRL WITH
THREE
BIRTHDAYS

**An Adopted Daughter's Memoir
of Tiaras, Tough Truths, and Tall Tales**

PATTI EDDINGTON

SHE WRITES PRESS

Published 2024
Printed in the United States of America
Print ISBN: 978-1-64742-650-7
E-ISBN: 978-1-64742-651-4
Library of Congress Control Number: 2023915576

For information, address:
She Writes Press
1569 Solano Ave #546
Berkeley, CA 94707

Interior Design by Tabitha Lahr

She Writes Press is a division of SparkPoint Studio, LLC.

For my beloved parents Jim and Millie Eddington, and for baby Mary Ann as well.

I can see the future, and everything is going to turn out just fine.

PREFACE

A memoir is a story told from one person's perspective based on that person's memories.

As a journalist, it was difficult for me at times to tell just one side of this story—mine—and I often asked for opinions on these events from others. In almost all cases, I allowed those I talk about to read what I wrote. For that reason, it was unnecessary for me to change many names. I did change the identities of a few people to protect their families.

It was a difficult decision for my editors and myself to reproduce the excerpts from the Report of Investigation verbatim—with errors in punctuation, inconsistent abbreviations, and strikethroughs—but we ultimately did to allow the reader to experience the document exactly as I did when it fell from that manila envelope. It had been created by a busy court worker on a manual typewriter several years before Wite-Out was invented.

In the report I am referred to as both Mary Ann, which was my birth name, and Patty instead of Patti; I changed that spelling myself when I was a teenager.

Chapter 1

HERE'S THE THING
ABOUT THE TRUTH

For more than fifteen years, I believed the tale I was told by an older half-sister I didn't meet until I was in my forties. She said I became a ward of the court at only three days old. I was living with my biological mother, Lois, and four siblings in an unheated garage with no plumbing when a social worker came, banged on our rickety door, and took me away.

"I ran after the car and kicked the tires and cried, 'Give us back our baby,'" said my sister, who was a little girl of only ten at the time.

I'm sure that's what she remembered. I know that's what she believed. But recently, a decade and a half after I first heard *that* story, a newly discovered aunt—the sister of my biological father—told me there had been a knock on *her* family's door, and when they answered, Lois thrust me, wrapped in a soiled and frayed blanket and possibly slightly injured, into *their* arms and said, "Here. If you want her, you can have her."

It was easy to imagine a poignant scene: Lois setting out on her journey on a winter night in 1960 dressed maybe in a threadbare coat and a babushka, carrying me across broken sidewalks, passing the homes of happier families who sat in the white glow of their living room televisions and watched *The Huntley/Brinkley Report* or *77 Sunset Strip*.

Except when I asked my new aunt for the address of the home where her family was living at the time and did a Google Earth search, I found it was *far* outside of the town. Lois couldn't have walked.

This is my story and I've tried to tell the truth. But I've learned the truth is malleable. We all want to tell either the prettiest—or maybe sometimes the most grotesque—of tales.

One other thing I've learned can affect the truth greatly—the passage of time. Time, I've come to find, is very, very good at deception. It is almost as good as people.

Chapter 2

BEAUTY LESSON

The realization hit after I'd spent decades parroting the only story I knew. When understanding finally dawned, I lurched on the heated table violently; Jackie, the lash extension lady hovering six inches above my upside-down face, could have dropped her pointy tweezers in my eye. I'd been describing the first photograph of me in my childhood photo album. I wore a stiffly starched dress, ruffled anklets, and tiny, orthopedic shoes. Our collie mix, Joe, rested at my feet at the base of the towering maple tree in front of our old farmhouse. It was 1961, so the photo was black and white. I knew, because my mother later told me, my tightly curled halo of hair was tinted red, the result of a Tonette perm and a henna rinse.

I was only twenty months old but Mom, a beautician with a head full of bottle-blonde, cotton candy curls, said the ministrations were necessary. She said I'd been maltreated in the foster home where I first lived after I'd been given up for adoption.

"Your hair was so fine and lifeless, I decided to cut it all off and give you some color and body," she said.

It made sense. After many years of foster kids and a previously failed adoption attempt, Mom was hopeful she might soon have her own little forever-kid, and she'd want me to be as fashionable as she was. That story was normally part of my repertoire when describing my stubborn, eccentric, overprotective mother. Sometimes I switched it out with the tale of the time she gave ten-year-old me a sex ed talk while driving to church or the incident when she grabbed one of her misbehaving chickens around the neck and tossed it in the outhouse to give it time to "settle down."

My stories about Millie were always sweetly received, which is exactly what I wanted. As much as *I* loved her, I knew she often needed some good PR.

It was easier telling stories about my dad, who was bald, handsome, sweet-natured, generous, and funny. He was always plowing the driveways of the widows on our road, or scooping up coleslaw for the Friday Night Lions Club Fish Fry, or transporting human eyes in a cooler from the big hospital in Lansing to the eye bank in Ann Arbor. I know the last sounds odd, but in the 1970s, it was allowed. Dad would go to a hospital in Lansing or Flint, pick up a carefully wrapped, shoebox-sized parcel packed into a cooler with ice bags, and drive it an hour and a half to the destination. He did this after a 5:00 a.m. wake-up call and eight-hour workday, getting home at 8:00–9:00 p.m., going to bed, and starting all over again.

Mom was a harder sell. My older cousins remembered her smacking their knuckles with a butter knife if their table manners were lacking. They were *always* lacking, by the way. She was a big-city transplant, opinionated and outspoken, politically minded, a take-no-prisoners, larger-than-life personality who landed in the cornfields of mid-Michigan in 1950 after marrying my father.

Noting Mom's peplum suits, French manicures, Lana Turner pompadour, and weighing the vast differences between her liberal Protestant daughter and conservative Catholic son-in-law, my grandmother told Mom she'd see her back in Detroit within twelve months. Accepting the challenge, our five-foot-two firebrand pulled on some overalls, shoveled chicken shit, and lived amid those cornfields for the next fifty-seven years, never forgetting her red Max Factor lipstick.

My stories about Millie were meant to soften the hard edges, show her truly charming side, and entice everyone else into loving her as much as I did.

Even though decades had passed, and my eyelash lady worked in an upscale salon in our Lake Michigan resort town while Mom practiced her beauty treatments in a damp laundry room overlooking a cow pasture, I thought Jackie might get a kick out of the "perm and henna on a toddler" story.

She did. But just like the time people laughed at what I thought was a poignant moment during a eulogy I was giving, her response was something I'd never considered.

"Oh, I get it," Jackie said. "You were in disguise."

Chapter 3

A PRETTY DRESS
AND PROBATE COURT

Cork Road, just outside the rural town of Morrice—
population just over one thousand even today—was
heavily settled by followers of the Catholic faith. They had
immigrated from Ireland during the potato famine of the
1840s, apparently traveling from Ellis Island to plop down
in the middle of the Michigan mitten.

In the 1960s, there were just five homes at the far
end of our dirt road. It originated about eight miles south
and meandered through corn and wheat fields, crossing
three paved, two-lane roads until it ran into I-69 at the
turnaround near the house where I grew up. In summer,
wildflowers grew tall against fading barns and roadside
silos, and beautiful orange-and-black orioles—so abundant
the high school mascot was the oriole—flitted along the
fence rows.

A pair of grandparents lived closest to the turnaround,
in a peeling farmhouse. But younger families resided in the
other homes, which were also old and juxtaposed oddly with

my family's new, modern, redbrick ranch. There were eight parents in those four houses—dads who worked on their farms or in a factory and moms who cooked and cleaned and hung laundry on clotheslines—until I reached high school, when the number fell to six after two scandalous, messy divorces. There were also twenty kids under those few roofs, aged infant to surly teenager.

An average of five children for four homes may already seem like a lot, but consider this: I was an only child. The other three families were *more* than doing their part to populate the countryside. My neighbor kids got up at 5:00 a.m. to tend to their cows, played HORSE with a mostly deflated ball and a rusty hoop without a net, drank milk out of the carton while standing in front of the open refrigerator, and ate butter-and-sugar sandwiches on gooey white Wonder Bread for lunch. They were athletic and wiry and free, sunburned and beautiful in a scraped-up knee, tangled-hair, country-kid kind of way. I was a pudgy, near-sighted bookworm with perennially misbuttoned shirts, parents who cared too much, an insatiable reading habit, and a tendency to be dramatic.

When I was eight, my mother told me to gather my shorts and sleeveless tops and begin packing my pink, plastic suitcase for a spring break trip to Florida. She found me, instead, perched on the corner of my chenille-covered double bed staring into our apple orchard and tearfully waving goodbye to our herd of beef cattle. It wasn't a cheery, "See you in ten days, dear cow friends" goodbye but more of a "I'm sure we're going to die in a horrific crash with a semi-truck carrying a load of head lettuce, and you'll be shipped off to be served as steak even *sooner*" forlorn wave.

Mom reminded me of two things: Dad was a very good driver, and I always overreacted. Ironically, I was mimicking her own over-the-top behaviors and eccentricities.

One example was Millie's church attire, which was frequently a mink stole with her monogram stitched in script on the creamy, taupe, satin lining. She'd purchased it as a young woman while she worked at Hudson's Department Store in downtown Detroit, and it was her prize possession. Perched high atop her platinum curls, she balanced a burnt orange, felt hat with a large pheasant feather on the right side. She wore the combo almost every Sunday in the fall as she and I headed off the fourteen miles on country roads in our latest Oldsmobile 88. The make and model were my father's passion, and he bought a new one every year.

We were going to St. John's United Church of Christ in the "big city" of Owosso. Dad had already attended mass at St. Mary's in uptown Morrice, then had his fill of buttermilk pancakes, maple syrup, and bacon and settled into his maroon, brushed-velvet La-Z-Boy recliner with the Detroit Free Press. I loved Mom's hat, but it was also a trauma whenever she wore it because she would instruct me to turn the car visor against my passenger-side window "so some dumb hunter doesn't mistake me for a bird and shoot me in the head."

She also showed me how to take control of the steering wheel and gently ease the car to the side of the road in case she ever had a coronary while driving. She'd been diagnosed with an enlarged heart as a child and sent to a special "fresh air" school, where she was fed porridge and made to sit outdoors in the sunshine to stay healthy. While her condition didn't seem to instill much caution during her daredevil childhood years, as she aged, she apparently began to live in fear one day her heart would sputter to a stop while alone with me in the car.

Millie couldn't pass on her small, delicate hands or infectious laugh, but clearly, she tutored me well in drama.

So, it's not surprising when I parked outside the 116-year-old Shiawassee County Courthouse and clicked my key fob on a frigid Friday in January 2020, the monologue swirling in my head was passionate and overly theatrical.

Here I am. About to walk up the same steps *Mom and Dad took when they finalized my adoption. The* same steps *Lois took when the judge rescinded her maternal rights.*

Of course, it's possible Lois wasn't even in the room as I became a ward of the court in December 1960 when I was only thirteen months old—or maybe fourteen depending on which of my birth certificates you choose to believe. It is likely she was not there. From what I was learning, jurisdiction over her five children didn't seem to be a priority with my biological mother.

Whatever happened, I thought, taking a moment to admire the sweeping majesty of the courthouse and its towering cupola, *this building played probably the* most *integral role of any building in my life.*

The gray-haired sheriff's deputy, who put my cell phone in a tiny locker and my purse through the metal detector, was so kind and solicitous I almost blurted out, "I'm here to see if I can get my adoption record unsealed and find out what in the actual hell happened way back then."

"Where can I direct you, ma'am?"

"Probate court, please."

"Oh," he said sympathetically, "you're in the wrong place."

Of course I was. Why would this visit be any less a red herring than the rest of the twisty, disturbing story I'd begun patching together? I slogged back to my car to head across the big parking lot to the correct building and thought about driving on to find a cup of coffee or a good bookstore, finally putting my past in the past. The few friends and relatives I'd told about this quest had looked concerned and gently asked me why and especially why now, after all this time?

For years, I'd been telling them I had no interest in finding out what happened during the first twenty months of my life. That had all changed, though, with the results of a simple DNA spit test I'd received as a gift from my daughter and the look in my new Aunt Eva's eyes when we met not even two years earlier. After all those decades in denial, I'd tapped into the Human Genome Project, sent off a vial filled with my saliva, and a couple months later opened an email that unfurled decades of mystery, answering a few questions but posing many more.

Just two weeks after receiving my results, I sat beside my diminutive newly discovered aunt at a quinceañera as she hugged me, patted my cheek, and stroked my arm.

"You were living with me and my sister Jane and her husband Cecil in the house they bought because we were all going to be a family, honey. But one day Jane dressed you up in your pretty dress and put a bow in your hair. I said, 'Where are you taking our baby? Where are you taking . . . Mary?'" Aunt Eva's eyes misted. "And Jane said, 'We have to take Mary to see a judge, but when we come home, she will be ours forever and ever.' But then . . . we never saw you again."

Chapter 4

LIKE JAGGED CONFETTI

Once they decided to adopt, it took a very long time for my parents to find a child. By then, they were almost as old as the *grandparents* of most of my friends—Mom was forty-eight and Dad forty-five when I started kindergarten. I don't remember being told I was adopted; it was just something I always knew.

"We chose you because you were the cutest little girl in the cabbage patch," my mother would say, which, of course, made me feel happy and special.

My adoptee status was something I wore like my cozy, pink, angora sweater—it was as much a part of my persona as my dark-brown, wavy, and unruly hair. But it wasn't something I ever imagined anyone else would give a damn about.

Then one Friday at recess in the sixth grade, I sat on a swing next to a classmate I'd never played with before. Dragging our white Keds in the dirt, I told her how excited I was for my uncle Frank's wedding the next day.

At sixty, my father's previously unmarried older brother had found the love of a no-nonsense, devout Catholic woman named Margaret, who resembled the photos I'd seen in the *Encyclopedia Britannica* of Eleanor Roosevelt. There would be a rehearsal dinner that night, and then we would go out to dinner at a *fancy* seafood restaurant where I would be allowed to order butterfly shrimp and a kiddie cocktail instead of my usual burger basket with fries and chocolate milk. I had a new cotton mini-dress in a psychedelic orange-and-pink paisley print and a matching over-the-shoulder cloth purse with a gold tone chain for the wedding. That trendy dress, playing with the most popular girl in school . . . I didn't think I'd ever been happier.

"It all sounds so fun," she said. "You know, I actually *really* like you. You're very nice."

"You're nice, too," I replied, giddily.

"My mother told me never to play with you, though," she added, beginning to pump her swing high. "She said you don't live with your real parents."

My heart beat faster. I felt my cheeks redden, and I ran off the playground and through the long school hallway to the restroom, slammed the door to a stall, sat on the toilet seat, and scrunched my knees to my chest. People, *adult* people, were talking about *me* in their homes. My throat tightened but I didn't cry. I knew I hadn't done anything wrong, but I was still embarrassed.

Years later I realized what I was really feeling as I hid in the bathroom stall until the teacher sent a classmate to look for me—shame.

I was only eleven, but I already understood it would be painful to my parents if I tried to delve into my origins, so I began to stuff down my natural curiosity. Like virtually all adoptions of the time, mine was "closed." The details of my biological family were intended to remain forever a secret, which I decided was just fine with me. I told myself I had no curiosity about anything before the photo with Joe the dog in front of the old maple.

For decades it remained that way. If someone asked if I knew who my *real* parents were, I would reply, "Absolutely," cock an eyebrow, narrow my eyes, and glare until they began to sputter their apologies.

When I was twenty-four and working at one of my first jobs as a journalist at the *Holland Sentinel* in western Michigan, an Associated Press reporter I knew named Linda—also an adoptee—asked if she could interview me for a series she was writing on the topic. Linda was probably ten years older, hard-nosed, brittle, and completely nonplussed by my insistence I had no real curiosity about my earliest days.

"For *every* adopted kid, the first thing that ever happened to them is they were *rejected*, and I can't *believe* you don't have more questions about where you came from," she groused. I insisted I didn't, even though I knew some of those closest to me were fascinated and couldn't understand how I didn't want to unravel the mystery.

It was during the same stint at the *Sentinel* where I met the woman who would become my surrogate sister, the free-spirited Thelma to my cautious Louise, my best friend, Kristen.

My high school boyfriend Jim and I had gotten married in 1981 while we were still college students at Michigan State University. I had just one more year to go in my undergrad journalism program, and Jim had two more years left in veterinary school. We spent the next couple years finishing our education, then working at poorly paid and unfulfilling first jobs. I worked at two small weekly newspapers, and he worked for a blowzy, cartoonish, Ann Arbor veterinarian, who warned Jim after a barbecue held to welcome him to never bring me into her clinic when she wasn't there because "she might steal something."

I'd been accused of being an ice queen, reserved, and a Pollyanna, but no one had ever said I looked like a thief. Her distrust of me was the least of her offenses. Jim suffered and struggled along for seven months before accepting an offer in January 1984 to work as an equine vet for a large practice outside of Grand Rapids. I landed the job at the Holland paper, about forty minutes away near the shores of Lake Michigan.

A few weeks earlier, I'd traveled to the lakeshore for my interview from a friend's apartment in downtown Grand Rapids, but by the time I started work, we'd rented a condo in the suburbs on the opposite side of the city. Remember, Siri didn't exist in 1984.

"Just go the same way you drove when you went for the interview," Jim told me.

Jim is a brilliant human and normally gives great advice.

"Don't mix your liquors" was one nugget I'd learned to respect very much, for example.

But as a young man, he disdained consulting a map or asking for directions. I once followed him around downtown Lansing for an hour searching for a mechanic located approximately five minutes from our tiny apartment. Still, I was twenty-four and very in love and apparently even more stupid. I *did* listen to him and backtracked miles out of my way to get on the same highway I'd used before and ended up fifteen minutes late for my first day on the job.

I'd worn cheap high heels, a polyester suit, and fake pearls, and as I slipped and slid across the icy parking lot, I looked up to see a petite blond with a pixie haircut and wearing an old bellboy's jacket and jeans hurrying in late as well. She gave me a huge welcoming smile and told me she'd been on the job as a photojournalist for exactly one week. Since she was also tardy, I felt a little better about being late.

Kristen was a joyous sprite who fit easily into the punk rock era of the mid-1980s. She was extraordinarily beautiful and fun-loving, her huge brown eyes often rimmed in kohl. She wore oversized men's wool coats and funky outfits she put together from thrift store finds and there was often a clove cigarette in her hand. Her shorn hair was sometimes spiked and occasionally rainbow hued. She drove a little shell-pink Toyota Corolla adorned with Dead Kennedys and Violent Femmes bumper stickers and was the object of much swooning from many of the men in the newsroom and likely a few of the women.

We worked well on assignments together, but she seemed too cool for me and way out of my friend league. When I first arrived at the *Sentinel*, I'd tried to forge an alliance with a nice, slightly built, very pale fellow reporter about my age named Kathy. I invited her to Grand Rapids one Saturday afternoon for shopping and lunch, but she was allergic to all makeup, most fabrics, and many foods. It was a long, stilted, forced afternoon. I thought about trying again, but as I was about to stop and ask her to grab a bite one day, I saw her desk was covered in discarded tissues—severe allergies—and decided to take myself out for a tuna melt sandwich at Big Boy and a half hour with a good book.

Shortly after, I was surprised when Kristen asked *me* to lunch. We ate at a small diner in nearby Zeeland and talked so long we were late getting back to work.

We haven't stopped talking for almost four decades.

I don't remember when I first told Kristen I was adopted. Maybe it was over our monthly piña coladas (me) and margaritas (her) at a Lake Michigan waterfront restaurant called The Hatch before I went to cover a Monday evening Holland board of education meeting. Whenever I mentioned it to her, it must have been early on because my memories of our friendship have always included her gazing at me, analyzing my high cheekbones, and speculating about my biology.

I traversed the West Michigan countryside in the early years of my career. I left the *Sentinel* to work for the *Grand Rapids Press* and the *Muskegon Chronicle* and then took a public relations job at a big hospital in Grand Rapids before opening WordStudio, my writing and publication design business. However, Kristen had only three jobs in her entire career. She worked at the *Holland Sentinel* before moving on to writing and editing positions at academic research institutions first at the University of Michigan medical center in Ann Arbor and then Fred Hutchinson Cancer Center in Seattle. She'd moved to the Emerald City after her first marriage dissolved, and she went to visit a former friend she'd worked with at U of M. She married the friend, Mark, in 1997.

I'd met her new husband a few times, most notably when I was maid of honor at Kristen's *first* wedding and he was a guest, and then of course, at their own beautiful celebration at a 1920s era inn in Saginaw. Kristen must have mentioned my background to him. In a meeting one day, he found himself fascinated by another attendee, a women's health nurse manager named Barb. He told Kristen he thought it was possible he found my biological sister; our looks were so similar.

A few weeks later, Barb contacted Mark for help with a project. He invited her to lunch and Kristen tagged along where she says they eventually confessed to poor befuddled Barb, who was likely mystified and possibly perturbed, but certainly not my sister.

I understand why Mark and Kristen behaved that way, though. Many years later, shortly after I'd learned about the whereabouts of some of my biological siblings but hadn't yet made a connection, I stopped for gas one day in DeWitt, a small town outside of the state capitol of Lansing, where

I'd heard one of my sisters lived. I'd seen no photos of her, but when a middle-aged woman pulled in beside me to fill up and smiled, I stared. Her crooked grin was so familiar. And weren't her eyes blue like mine? And wasn't this DeWitt? Obviously, the woman was no more related to me than Barb.

In retrospect, I realized there were clues my parents always had information about my identity. Scattered like jagged confetti throughout the years, there were little hints I could have picked up and tossed around to see where they'd land if I'd thought to try and if I'd actually *wanted* to dig at the truth; my birthday was an example.

Until I was fifteen, we'd celebrated on November 20. It was a magical date because it was also the birthday of an older boy who lived in my neighborhood. I'd initially become enamored of him simply because when I was four and he was five or six, my mother told me he'd tossed a note tied to a rock to profess his affection over our apple orchard fence. I've never been sure he really did, but it was enough for me to declare undying love (to everyone except him) and maintain a crush for several years.

Any future love story was abruptly aborted one summer afternoon when I was about seven. He challenged me to a game of chicken on our rickety bicycles. Too dumb to give in, I peddled down our bumpy dirt road as fast as my dimpled legs could take me, racing so close to him I could see his beautiful, big eyes through his thick glasses until he finally screamed out, "You moron," swerved, and crumpled into the ditch, scraping his leg, probably bruising his ego, and ending any hopes of a future relationship.

During the summer I was fifteen, I spent several weeks riding my black-and-tan, 10 speed John Deere bicycle two miles from our house to Morrice High School to sit in a classroom and watch scary movies about car crashes in driver's training. Most of us country kids had done time in the seat of the family tractor and a little blood and gore didn't deter even one of us from itching to get behind the wheel. I gave pause, though, when the instructor told us about the paperwork we'd need to get our learner's permit. Among other things, we'd need our birth certificates.

My mother was puttering in the kitchen when I approached her nervously. She was preparing our usual summertime "diet" lunch of cottage cheese and canned peaches while I made my request, apologizing and promising I wouldn't look at the name listed on it for me or the names of my birth parents.

Mom handled the matter breezily, though. "Oh, it's not a problem, honey," she said. "They actually redo your birth certificate when you are adopted. We have one with your new name and our names on it."

She left it for me on the tan, metal desk in my bedroom a few days later. Sure enough, the certificate listed my name as Patricia Ann Eddington and my parents as James and Mildred Eddington. There was no weight or length or tiny inked footprint, but there was a birthdate: November 15, 1959.

"Mom!" I said, dashing into the kitchen. "They got my birthday *wrong by five days* on my birth certificate!"

"Well," she replied, haltingly, "I didn't want any of those nosy old biddies who work at the hospital trying to figure out who you were. So, I adjusted the day you were born a little bit."

She asked me what I wanted to do and how I wanted to celebrate, since I now knew the actual date of my birth. It was 1975. I had been transfixed by the Watergate Hearings and Richard Nixon's downfall. Woodward and Bernstein were my idols, and I'd already decided I wanted to be a journalist. I told her I wanted to be truthful in *all* things, and henceforth I would celebrate on my *real* birthdate.

She nodded solemnly and agreed.

At about the same time Mom brought me my birth certificate, I became transfixed by the Truman Capote book *In Cold Blood*, which detailed the murders of the Clutter family in a farmhouse in Holcomb, Kansas. It was an instant runaway best seller when it was published in 1966, and I read it over and over when I was in high school. I loved the journalistic/fiction style Capote brought to a nonfiction story, but the book was meaningful to me in another way as well. It described the murders in horrifying detail and set out the timeline and date of the crime, which took place early in the morning of Sunday, November 15, 1959.

Today you could do a quick Google search to find out what day of the week any date fell on, but such research wasn't so easy in the 1970s. I felt like such an investigative reporter uncovering the truth.

"I found out I was born on a Sunday from reading *In Cold Blood*," I would tell people. I thought it was interesting in a macabre kind of way.

I would be fifty-eight years old before I learned I wasn't born November 15, either.

Chapter 5

DADDY-O

....

Father: *James Eddington is a tall, thin man. He is getting quite bald, but he has dark hair and brown eyes. He is a friendly man, but seems to be somewhat reserved. He has a speech difficulty and stutters sometimes.*

Mr. Eddington has been employed by Oldsmobile as an Inspector for 12 years. He also farms his farm. Much of his land was taken by the new highway that went through on his property, so that he has less land to farm now. He raises Herefords, at the present time he has ~~seventeen~~ fourteen head.

—Taken directly from the Report of Investigation re: Patricia Ann Eddington, (Mary Ann Ball), April 2, 1962. File No. 693— (Mrs. Barbara Trezise, Court Worker)

....

Though he would never have described himself this way, my father was an *elegant* man. A quality control manager at the Oldsmobile plant in Lansing thirty minutes from our home—his job was painstaking. He pulled cars randomly from the assembly line and went over them inch by inch, placing little yellow adhesive arrows pointing to tiny defects or dings invisible to the ordinary eye. He also spent much of his career driving the 88s and 98s and the sexy, sporty, non-Oldsmobile-like 442s on the Lansing highways, circling the state capitol rotunda and listening intently for slight rumbles, clicks, or hums—any small indication of a less-than-perfect machine.

Driving with Dad in your car always meant at some point you would have a conversation about the state of your (always faulty) vehicle.

DAD: "Do you hear that?"
HAPLESS DRIVER: "No?"
DAD: "Shhh. Listen carefully."
HAPLESS DRIVER: "I don't hear—"
DAD: "Pull over."

He loved the perfectionism necessary for his job. It was the way he lived all aspects of his life, and he took great pride in his work and his world being pristine. His dark-brown work pants might be worn shiny and thin at the knees, but Mom pressed them with a sharp crease. She also ironed his monogrammed "hankies," and he carefully placed a white plastic pen holder in the pocket of his flannel or poplin shirt each morning in case of a ballpoint mishap.

In addition to his factory work, Dad was also a gentleman farmer. Once the proud owner of 150 acres, most of his land was condemned in the late 1950s when the state cut through his property to build the I-69 thoroughfare connecting Lansing and Flint. Dad stood on principle and refused to sell, so the government condemned his land, leaving him with just thirty-nine acres and paying him a fraction of their initial offer. He wore that story of stubborn dissent as a badge of honor and pride even though by the time I was eight or nine, he was raising just forty head of Herefords and renting out most of his property to the dairy farmer across the street who used it to plant corn.

When she moved to Morrice, my mother gave up her hairdressing career to raise chickens and a slew of foster children, the last being me.

Theirs was a unique pairing for the time.

Dad grew up poor on a farm a few miles outside of Morrice. "Don't blink or you'll miss it," he would always tell people when describing the village. He joked about its size, but he loved our little burg with a fierce intensity. His own father died after a long battle with cancer when Dad was only fifteen. The family barely weathered the Great Depression, surviving on the largesse of small-town community kindness and the upstanding reputation the Eddington name held.

"They had so many bills when his father died," my mother told me, recounting the stories her husband had bashfully shared with her when they started dating. "But your father paid off every last bit of it, little by little. That's the kind of man he is."

Dad could bring me to tears, telling me about the time his sweet and shy mother, Mary wanted to treat her three kids and gave them some of her precious script to go to the movies. They were turned away at the door of the theater and told to come back when they had real money.

"Buddy, don't take it so hard," he would say to me every time I began weeping when he told the story. "Look, I got over it." He might have, but I never did.

"You're so tenderhearted," my mother would often say to me. It wasn't a compliment.

A bout of scarlet fever when he was ten left my father with a speech impediment so severe, the bullying ultimately led him to flee the Catholic school in Lansing where his mother moved after his father died to live with his uncle who was a priest in Adrian seventy-five miles away. While there, the uncle—Father Peter Jordan—sent him to a summer camp in Northport on the scenic Leelanau Peninsula, where he made huge strides in overcoming his impediment. While I was a child, he still used a tapping method, making the "okay" sign, then flicking his forefinger to a tabletop repeatedly and rhythmically when he struggled to speak.

"Never, ever interrupt your father or finish a word for him," Mom cautioned me, and whenever an unknowing or dim friend did, she arched her eyebrow at them in warning.

He often struggled to speak, but Dad had a gorgeous singing voice and never once stuttered when he sang. Our car trips were filled with his beautiful, melodious tenor, and I asked every time for him to treat us to "Shine on Harvest Moon" and "When Irish Eyes Are Smiling." He always finished his mini concert with "The Old Grey Mare" so he could hear me giggle and sing along with him.

"She oomped on the whiffletree."

He replaced "kicked" with "oomped" and told me it meant pooped, so I was convinced I was singing something incredibly naughty. Ironically, as he aged and almost without our notice, Dad's speech gradually improved, and my friends who met him when I was an adult were surprised he'd ever stuttered.

In elementary school, I would run to meet Dad the minute his truck pulled up our long gravel driveway each afternoon. I wasn't the only one. My dog, Queenie, a lovable and scruffy mutt Dad brought home when I was four, always beat me to greet him, moving from her spot on the front porch at exactly 3:15 p.m. to sit under the big trees in our front yard. She watched for the cloud of dust, which kicked up as his Chevy quarter-ton pickup truck made its way down Cork Road.

Dad rose to the ear-shattering, heart-piercing clang of his Big Ben alarm clock each weekday morning at 5:00 a.m., often waking me as well. My room was directly adjacent to his. I never remember my parents sleeping in the same room. My mother was a lifelong insomniac and would doze off on one of our two couches in front of the TV each night while watching Johnny Carson. Dad would often wake, stumble out into the living room to turn off the glare of the test pattern only to have her rouse and grumble, "I was watching that!"

Don't misunderstand, though; there was a lot of love in my parents' marriage. They might not have shared a bed, but once a week or so, when I was small, they'd turn on a *Tom and Jerry* or *Mighty Mouse* cartoon and tell me they'd be back as soon as Mom shampooed Dad's hair in the basement washtub. I was in college before I remembered his, "God only made so many perfect heads and the rest he covered with hair" baseball cap and all the times he told people he was lucky because he could shampoo his nearly bald head with a bar of soap and a washrag. That's when I recalled their half-hour "shampoo" sessions and remembered the basement had two couches.

Most mornings when I heard Dad wake up, I'd get up and peek into his bedroom to see him sitting slumped on the edge of the bed, forehead in his palm, girding himself for another long day. While he washed up—we wouldn't have a shower until I was in high school and then one of those ridiculous handheld sprayers—Mom got up, donned her robe, and made him a fried egg with toast or a bowl of oatmeal. She'd pack his metal lunchbox with a sandwich and a couple of homemade cookies and brew hot tea for his thermos. She let it cool before she'd painstakingly melt ice cubes under running water until they could fit in the opening of the container so he could have iced tea with his lunch.

When he'd leave, she'd head back to her couch. By the time I was in second or third grade, she expected me to do my own wash up, pour my own cereal, dress in the clothes she'd laid out the night before, then wait quietly by the front window. I'd watch for my school bus, which would pass our house on the way to the turnaround, then rumble its way back up the street.

I'd let myself out the front door and walk to the end of our long driveway, hoping I'd find an easy seat amid my noisy, roughhousing peers when the yellow Blue Bird bus pulled up.

o o o

Farm people often ate dinner early, and even though Dad was mostly not a farmer, our dinner was still always at 5:00 p.m. The table was set with a small platter of meat (normally a hamburger or steak from one of our own Herefords), potatoes (baked or mashed), and a small slab of iceberg lettuce topped with French or thousand island dressing. It was a popular salad of the day, and many years later Jim would sigh heavily when our young daughter Molly would order the exact same dish at a fancy restaurant for twelve dollars. Growing up, there was always a stack of Michigan-made Koepplinger's white bread, while I longed for the cheaper, moist Wonder Bread the neighbor kids ate, placed in front of my father with a hunk of Land O'Lakes butter.

It varied but there was *always* something sweet to end the meal, and it was frequently home baked. Ours were calorie-laden dinners, which were fine for my active, six-foot, 180-pound, wiry father but dangerously pudge-making for a little girl. Those dinners were probably the main reason Mom and I always did penance by eating our "diet" lunches of cottage cheese and canned peaches during the summer.

There were few weeknights when Dad stayed home after we ate. He was perennially elected to the Morrice School Board and those meetings were held on Monday night. On Wednesdays his Lions Club held bingo night at the Morrice Community Hall, and on Fridays there was frequently a fish fry at Lions Club Park. Then there were St. Vincent de Paul and Knights of Columbus meetings once a month and sometimes evening Mass.

On nights when Dad ate at the fish fry, Mom and I would dine daringly and exotically, opening cans of LaChoy Chicken Chow Mein or a box of Kraft Tangy Italian Spaghetti. It was food Dad would never try, and we felt a little decadent and wild enjoying it without him.

They still sell that green and white and red Kraft spaghetti dinner, and occasionally our family will buy a box so we can have "Grandma spaghetti" and let my heart break a little.

Once a month, Mom would have her Morrice Women's Club meeting, one of several of *her* service organizations, and Dad and I would make the trip to Lansing and Uncle John's Pancake House where he allowed me to order a big stack of chocolate chip flapjacks covered in whipped cream.

I sometimes wondered why my parents fought so long and hard to adopt a child when I remember so many times being alone with one or the other and not together as a family unit. But then I remembered all of the vacations and weekend trips to the cottage at Town Line Lake, which my folks bought when I was ten. The little, white-and-yellow, two-bedroom dwelling perched on a hillside overlooking the small, inland lake was only about an hour and a half from home, so we went almost every weekend in the summer and early fall. We took pontoon rides and went fishing, and I swam in the algae-filled water until my eyes were rimmed red.

Every Saturday night, we had bonfires and marshmallow roasts with the neighbors at the lake, making pies with white bread and cherry filling in a special metal pie iron. I realized as I got older what I experienced was typical parenting of the time in our socioeconomic group and part of the world. My parents had gotten *exactly* what they'd wanted and dreamed of: traditional parental roles and an ordinary, loving family of the 1960s and 1970s.

Mom taught me manners and tutored me with flash cards to try to improve my horrible math skills (it didn't work), and my father did his part to try to impart useful life lessons like how to change a tire and to never let the gas gauge on my first car (unsurprisingly an Oldsmobile 88 formerly belonging to Uncle Frank) get below a quarter tank.

"Dammit, Patti, not again!" he'd yell when for the tenth time I'd come to him admitting I was almost on empty and wouldn't make it to the Lansing suburbs for my job at Murphy's 5 & 10 in Meridian Mall the summer after I graduated from high school.

"Now you make *sure* this doesn't happen again, Buddy," he'd say, pointing his forefinger at me. "You *have* to be more responsible."

I'd always apologize and humbly agree, and he'd mutter a bit, then smile at me and head off to the gas house shaking his head but returning with a full orange metal gas can. Two or three weeks later the entire scene would play out again.

Except for the cringe-worthy time he warned me not to let a date take me to the "Durand Dirties," an X-rated drive-in movie theater, which was actually named The Scene (I was sixteen and didn't even know those kinds of movies existed), Dad's advice came more in the form of example—he led an exemplary life.

It has only been recently I realized not once in our almost fifty-year relationship did my father and I discuss my adoption.

Chapter 6

JUST HOW ARE YOU
GOING TO FIX *THAT?*

....

Mother: Mrs. Eddington is a woman of average height, and tends to be slightly plump. She has blond hair and blue eyes. She was born July 11 1916 in Detroit. She graduated from high school at the Commerce High School in Detroit.

Mrs. Eddington is much like Mr. Eddington in personality. She is friendly and cooperative but seems somewhat reserved. She appears to have a great love for children.

—Taken directly from the Report of Investigation re: Patricia Ann Eddington, (Mary Ann Ball), April 2, 1962. File No. 693—
(Mrs. Barbara Trezise, Court Worker)

....

Mom's family wasn't wealthy but fared better during the Great Depression and World War II than Dad's. Her gruff, German, immigrant father, Herman, was a driver for the fat cats at Kelsey-Hayes, an automotive parts plant in Plymouth. He died before I was born, and I never heard anything much about him except how taciturn he was. He must have been personable enough because the men he drove around gave him their extra gas rationing coupons and big tips. He and his wife, Anna, and their six children—the oldest two died before Mom was out of adolescence—had a bungalow-style home on prettily named Appoline Street on the south side of Detroit and a cottage at nearby Long Lake.

Mom was the third oldest, a slightly built tomboy imp with a mischievous grin. In photos, she resembled child actor Mary Badham, who played Scout Finch in the 1962 movie *To Kill a Mockingbird*. She swam, golfed with second-hand clubs, and one time broke into an abandoned cottage with some of her buddies and stole a wooden captain's chair. It later graced my childhood bedroom and has been painted and repainted and moved to a dozen of my apartments and homes. I still keep it as a reminder of the irrepressible character of the charming little girl who would become my mother.

She was a sun-kissed, ragtag urchin, disdaining the cadre of little boys who followed her around enamored by her spirit and apparently her cruelty. Her tonsils were removed on the kitchen table, and once she'd recovered, she dug through the trash to find the not-quite-empty can of ether the doctor had tossed out. She used it to chase a skinny and annoying young admirer named Sammy. She tackled him and forced him to inhale until he got woozy, and then she ran away giggling.

Though his stutter had caused so much pain in his life, Dad would have never met Mom without it. He showed up for his pre-enrollment army physical and was deemed 4-F because of his speech impediment. He opted to serve out the war years working at Kelsey-Hayes, where Mom's father drove those bigwigs and where Mom also worked in the office. The automotive parts supplier had been reconfigured to produce munitions during the war.

Though they'd seen each other around, Dad said he never dared talk to the petite blond and busty beauty. But his men's league bowling team followed her women's league team, and one night when he and his buddies sat in the lounge having a beer, she suddenly stood in front of him, tapping her toe impatiently.

"She said, 'Your car got stuck on my car. You need to come get it unhooked,'" he'd relate, obviously relishing the telling of the tale.

He followed her out to the street to find she'd pulled forward—until she quit driving at eighty-eight, she was iffy behind the wheel and was probably better described as a *dangerous* driver—and snagged her front bumper over his trailer hitch.

"There!" She pointed to the conjoined cars, accusingly. "Just how are *you* going to fix *that*?"

It was typical behavior of un-repentant Millie, who never enjoyed taking the blame for any of her actions. Once when I was eleven or twelve, shopping with Mom in her favorite fancy Owosso department store, Christians, she broke wind.

"Patti!" she hissed loudly, the corners of her mouth turning slightly up, her eyes twinkling. "For heaven's sake, where *are* your manners?"

She was adorable even if Dad or I had to frequently clean up after one of the messes she created.

"She didn't mean it *that* way, I'm sure. You just have to know her," we would stammer.

Once, Dad was left not only covering up a big mess she'd gotten into but burying the evidence as well. Shortly after they had moved to the country, he was at Mass one Sunday when, from the kitchen window, Mom saw a mangy, ebony tomcat from the farm across the road sneaking across the yard. It stalked her own beautiful and refined kitty, Fluffy, who was sunning herself on the grass. The stray obviously had romantic intentions, and it apparently wasn't the first time, since Fluffy had recently delivered one painfully oversized, black, stillborn kitten. Mom would be damned if the tom had the chance to act the Lothario again.

She knocked on the window and screamed, but the little Romeo couldn't be dissuaded so easily and continued slinking along toward dim, unaware Fluffy. Mom ran to the hall closet, got Dad's shotgun, and rushed to the front porch. The clattering of the screen door scared the wanderer, and he streaked past Mom full speed across our dirt road. She had never even held a gun before, but she raised it and took aim just as the would-be rapist leapt across a low fence in the ditch. I always felt bad hearing this.

"He was just looking for love," I told Mom.

"You're too tenderhearted," she'd reply.

Dad came home to his favorite breakfast of bacon and eggs and pancakes and the news that Mom had "a little job" for him.

"Goddamn it, Millie!" he yelled. Despite his utter devotion to his religion, "Goddamn it, Millie!" was a refrain I would hear from my father at least once a week every year of my childhood, though when he (infrequently) yelled at me he always left off "God." Then he stomped off across the road toward the field with a shovel.

"I never thought it would be dead," Dad always said, shaking his head in disbelief when he told the story. "I thought she'd just maimed the damn thing, and I would have to finish the job. But she got it all right. She got it midair."

Relatives often said Mom softened with the years. Instead of becoming tougher by farm living, she ultimately became more gentle and loving, and I think it's true. In her early days in the country, she told me she'd once had to drown a litter of premature puppies. I was horrified and ran to my room sobbing.

"They wouldn't have lived; they would have suffered. It was the kindest thing to do," she assured me. "Don't be so tenderhearted."

But aside from the poor neighbor cat, she loved animals, *especially* cats, and we always had at least one. When I was a child, we had two barn cats, Tommy and Pepper. The mangy little duo lived off mice and whatever scraps of bread and milk Mom would give me to take to them in a tin pie pan every evening. We always left the barn door slightly open so they could take shelter in bad weather.

The nine dogs and cats Jim and I have adopted throughout our marriage have lived in luxury—food in their bowls, snug in their own comfy beds, or nestled at the foot of ours. Our greyhound, Gabbi, a surprise gift for Jim's fiftieth birthday, had her own full-size couch in the sitting room off of our bedroom. She was so naturally thin and bony, she needed an extra bit of cushion, we reasoned.

As a kid, it never struck me my pets might not have had an easy time; it was the way of life on a farm. Queenie, as much as we loved her, was tied up on a long chain to her doghouse at night. The cats lived in the barn, burrowing into the straw when the snow blew and mostly fending for themselves twelve months a year.

I never thought about their lives until one Sunday night when I was in sixth grade, and we returned home from a weekend at the cottage. Dad went to check on my ponies, Susie and Star—the cows had been sold off. He came back grim-faced and whispered to my mother, who followed him out to the barn while I trailed along behind, unnoticed. The pony sitter had forgotten to leave the barn door cracked for the cats. Never a very good mouser, Tommy was still hovering around the door, meowing with hunger and dreaming of his pan of stale bread crusts and milk. But the more adventurous Pepper had tried to gain entry through a crack in the old building—a very narrow crack. From the outside, all that was visible was Pepper's swollen and distorted hindquarters. He'd gotten caught in the opening and strangled. My parents finally saw me and shooed me away before Dad dislodged his body, but it was a sad and graphic image I've obviously never forgotten.

Pepper's demise must have affected my parents as well because if you juxtapose his story with Toby's, the orange-and-white, long-haired tabby my folks got me as consolation for selling Susie and Star just a few years later, there was no comparison.

Selling my horses was one of the bigger traumas of my preteen life. I wasn't a typical, "I want a pony" girl, but I liked *every* animal. While Dad had been raised with pigs, chickens, and cows, he apparently had always wanted a horse.

A friend of his knew someone who knew someone, and when I was eight, we borrowed a trailer and traveled an hour to Grand Ledge to pick up Susie, a cantankerous, teenaged Welsh pony. Susie had already had several owners and didn't seem any more thrilled to be with us than she had been delighted to be with any of them. She'd head to the far corner of her pasture when a car with kids in the back seat pulled in the driveway, apparently thinking, "These assholes think they're going to ride me. Ha! I'll show them."

Once Dad had chased her around and around with her bridle and finally captured her, she'd puff out her big belly long enough for him to throw the saddle over her broad back, then wait for her prey. One of us kids was always brave or stupid enough to swing our leg up into the stirrup. Susie would snort, then take off, inhaling rapidly so the saddle swung under her stomach, normally dumping us into a nice warm pile of horse shit.

Dad borrowed the trailer again and took her back to Grand Ledge to have her bred by a palomino stallion named Reb, short for Rebel. The product of their union was a yellow colt with a white blotch on his forehead, halfway in size between Welsh pony and full-sized horse. I, not very creatively, named him Star.

Star was such a lovable idiot; he never even needed to be broken. Dad could easily put a bridle and saddle on him, and he would walk gently around the pasture like the ponies on the ring at the county fair. Susie was too edgy to ride, but Star was too boring.

Both ate their fill of oats, hay, sugar cubes, and carrots, and after about five years Mom and Dad sold them without telling me. I was inconsolable and hatched a plan to run away with them and live in the woods. When I realized I'd have to sleep outdoors and miss both *The Brady Bunch* and *The Partridge Family*, I consulted my life coach of the time—the Dial-a-Prayer phone number—and told Mom I'd concede.

"But could I get a cat?" I asked.

Toby was the first of my family's pets ever allowed *in* the house. After the Pepper tragedy, my parents relented a bit on the treatment of felines. In fair weather, Toby was allowed to roam freely and sleep either outdoors or indoors at his choosing but would not be provided a litter box. In the winter, he would have a box in the basement.

My cat grew obese from days of hunting mice followed by a nice Meow Mix dinner. Sometimes he lounged on a patio chair on the screened-in porch at the back of our house where he could survey the fields. And sometimes he spent hours sitting in the middle of Cork Road.

"Toby!" Mom would scream out the front screened door. "Get out of the road, you idiot!" Her recriminations had exactly the same effect on him as when she would

open the door as he sat under her bird feeder gazing hope-
fully upward and yell, "Toby! Eat the mice not the birds!
The mice not the birds!" In either case he would blink his
golden eyes slowly at her, turn back to survey his domain,
and remain exactly where he was.

Because he was my pet and my folks had all that "we
sold her ponies without telling her" guilt, Toby was allowed
to travel with us to the cottage each weekend. He would ride
in the back of Dad's truck with the topper along with Queenie,
our coolers of food, suitcases, and the toy of the season.

"Excuse me," a man at a gas station said, approaching
my dad as we stopped for a fill-up. "But is that a cat sitting
in there on a snowmobile?"

"Yes, it is," my father said. "But honestly, he prefers
our spring trips when he can ride on the motorcycle. He's
higher up. Better view."

Chapter 7

STUBBORN AND STOIC

It was likely my mother's ingrained German stoicism that was the root cause of the reserved nature the court worker noted in my adoption file. I was eight before I saw her cry.

My uncle Chester, who was married to my mother's younger sister, Esther, died on the surgery table while undergoing an open-heart procedure. Uncle Chet had been a favorite of mine. He taught me how to blow up a balloon. On a sun-dappled afternoon, when Star was just a few months old, Uncle Chet, a confirmed city slicker, slapped his knees and doubled over with laughter when Dad let my colt run loose in our side yard, kicking up his heels and farting resoundingly with every kick.

I'd been outside playing with my next-door neighbor and best friend, Clara, one day when I rushed in to use the bathroom and Mom told me Chet had died. She was sitting in her favorite rocking chair, rocking forward then back, dragging her bare feet slowly over the carpet. Tears slid down her cheeks, and there was a wadded-up tissue in her hands.

Mom is sad, I thought. It was the first time I realized such a thing was even possible. It was terribly frightening.

When she was in her mid-twenties, my daughter Molly and I were in the middle of a conversation I can't recall, but whatever I told her must have been embarrassing.

"Maybe I shouldn't have told you that," I mused. "I don't think my mother would have told me that sort of thing."

"But, Mom, you and I have a much closer relationship than you did with Grandma," Molly replied.

I'd never thought of my relationship with my mother as not close. I knew she loved me but until she was in her seventies, she never told me; it was just something she assumed could go unspoken. As I aged, I realized how lucky I'd been to have a front row seat, watching a woman who truly believed in herself and her rights and her power. At the time, though, her stubborn demeanor and eccentricities were frequently embarrassing.

When school let out each summer, my days revolved around Mom's predetermined schedule, which meant every Wednesday I dragged my feet after her on her shopping trips to Owosso. Located about fifteen minutes away from Morrice, it was one of only a few bona fide cities in Shiawassee County and had several grocery stores. Mom scoured the Owosso *Argus Press* each week to make sure she got the best bargains, then set out on a complicated route to visit at least three, sometimes four, stores in one day.

"I'm pretty sure your mother spends more in gas each week traipsing from place to place than she saves from clipping those coupons," Jim told me in later years.

It was probably true, but it didn't really matter because what she was really after was the win.

Shopping in Vescio's, a large, family-owned grocery store with distinctive black-and-white tile flooring perfect for a little girl to play hopscotch, Mom would inevitably pick up a pound of bacon and tear the cardboard cover away from the plastic-wrapped product so she could peek at the entire slab.

"Excuse me, ma'am!" another shopper said, tapping Mom on the shoulder one day, obviously furious. "What do you think you're doing? You're wrecking that package of bacon!"

"I'm not *wrecking* it, I'm *checking* it," Mom said, absolutely undisturbed by the woman's fury. "If it looks okay, I'll buy it, but I *won't* buy something I can't see."

Those shopping trips always ended in humiliation for me. I don't remember one instance when Mom didn't make the checkout boy repack every bag of groceries.

"You're crushing my bread. You need to put the canned goods on the bottom. Watch the fruit, you'll bruise it," she would say to the glowering, beet-faced teenager.

It wasn't that she was wrong, but it inspired anxiety in a little girl.

I didn't sleep for an entire night after a trip to the Shiawassee County Fair one August when Mom yelled at some 4-H kids in one of the livestock barns when they erupted into an impromptu water gun fight.

"Hey! You got me wet!" she yelled.

"You old bag!" a kid yelled back.

My father cocked his fist and turned around, but she grabbed his arm and said gently, "It's okay, Jim."

I cried silently in the car on the way home, looking lovingly at the back of my parents' heads and vowing never to go to the stupid fair again. I knew Mom could be outspoken and come across harshly, but what really bothered me was the boy had called her "old." My biggest fear was my parents would die and leave me alone. Had I been able to give voice to my pain, what I would have probably said was, "I'm afraid you will die and leave me alone . . . again."

Still, Mom's fortitude and self-confidence could also be inspiring.

Some of my earliest memories are of sitting on the floor of one of her friend's homes watching the vibrantly colored, "Kapow!" "Bam!" cartoon bubbles explode on the television screen as I watched the campy *Batman* show, while she and the few other activists in town had a meeting to plan their fight against consolidating our school district with the only slightly larger neighboring city of Perry.

"Perry is a suburb of Morrice, don't you forget it," my father always joked.

She'd sat on the board of education for Morrice Public Schools when the "schools" were a one-room structure. By the time I entered kindergarten in 1964, a new, modern building had been constructed, and Mom felt strongly that our little town needed to fight to retain its independence. She and her friends won their campaign.

Although the merger question has been on ballots a few times since, the issue is always defeated, and the districts remain separate.

As a teenager, I came home one day to find her in a fury about a phone call she'd made to one of our local legislators. Sitting on our high telephone stool at the kitchen counter, she'd dialed a lawmaker as he sat in session at the state capitol in Lansing to gripe about some issue.

"Madam!" he'd said. "I have no idea how you got my phone number here on the floor. But I cannot speak with you now. I am in session."

"Sir!" my mother replied. I've been to the capitol, and I've *seen* you in session. You have your feet on your desk, and you're reading the funnies. I think you have a moment to speak with me!"

As a child I could only fall asleep after Mom had listened to me recite the Lord's prayer, kissed me on the forehead, and left the door to my bedroom open so I could hear the sound of the television. If I awoke to use the bathroom in the middle of the night, I would creep into the living room to make sure she was there. Sometimes I would see her playing solitaire on the coffee table. If she couldn't win, she shuffled the cards from the bottom of the deck. Later, she would curl up on the sofa under an afghan she had created during her knitting phase. She also had a cake decorating phase and, many years later, an "I'm going to learn the ins and outs of these damn computers" phase.

In the mornings, she snored softly on her couch as I tried to pour my Cocoa Puffs or Fruity Pebbles as quietly as possible into my cereal bowl. She'd rouse slightly and wave goodbye when I eased open the door to leave.

I ached to stay with her, to run and have her hold me close, and to never leave.

Against her firm orders, I hardly ever washed my hands, and I chewed my fingernails obsessively, even though she painted them with a foul-tasting liquid to discourage me. I *wanted* my germ-laced fingers to make me sick. Catching a bad cold meant at least three days on the couch watching *The Andy Griffith Show* and *Bewitched* and hearing Mom puttering in the kitchen. It was heaven. As much as I longed to be with her, I wanted to be with her at *home*. Having Mom come to school always meant trouble.

In the mid-1960s, Morrice Public Schools had a sexist, arcane rule stating female students were not allowed to wear pants unless they wore them under a dress. It didn't matter if it was nineteen degrees and sleeting, no pants were allowed on the playground unless there was also a dress on top.

The rule was okay with me. Mom had a habit of almost always dressing me in a white blouse or sweater and red pants or skirt. I have no idea where it came from, but it inspired a lifelong aversion to red clothing in me. A stiffly starched plaid dress with a Peter Pan collar over polyester stirrup pants in any color but red was a look I coveted. I wanted to look like every other little girl on the monkey bars. Plus, the dress would cover my protruding stomach, while my stretch pants alone emphasized it. But day after day, no matter how I begged, Mom stubbornly sent me in pants.

"It's ridiculous, that's why," she sighed, in answer to my endless nagging. "It's not practical, that's why. Why should girls have to *do* that? That's why."

One day, when I came to school with a white wool sweater over my signature pants, I was sent to the office while the principal called my home and Mom came to the building. She winked and nodded at me as she walked by, and I sat terrified in one of the hard little chairs in the corner of his outer sanctum. When they emerged, he looked stricken and a bit pale and sent me back to class. I never knew what was said, but it was the last I personally heard of the "dress over pants" rule at Morrice Elementary School.

Once I passed my predictably snotty middle school years, Mom and I rarely fought. The episodes were so rare, I remember them vividly.

When I was between my freshman and sophomore years of college, looking for summer employment, my father suggested I get a job in the business office at the Oldsmobile plant. He was a beloved employee, and while he didn't say anything, I knew I'd get the job as long as I passed the mandatory typing test. But that was a problem.

My young and handsome high school typing teacher, Buck Heiney, was also the football coach. Buck graduated from college with a physical education major and a history minor, but he somehow also got stuck teaching mostly disinterested, Bazooka-smacking, sixteen- and seventeen-year-olds to type. I wish I could blame him for how lousy I was at the keyboard, but honestly, I was just an absolutely horrible typist.

In retrospect, "horrible" is probably a little too kind.

I'm sure Buck didn't love grading our "write a letter to a friend" assignments. Each time I'd write a mash note to my new boyfriend, Jim, and Buck would send them back to me with droll comments like, "You need to capitalize the 'F' in French." I think he also told me to be careful.

If the C I got in high school typing class wasn't enough to convince my parents, I wish we could have fast-forwarded a couple years to the fall of 1979 when I transferred from Lansing Community College to Michigan State University to major in journalism. The J school at MSU had an outdated rule that said to-be-admitted students had to first pass a sixty-word-per-minute typing test. I'd wanted to be a journalist since I was fifteen, and while I knew hard work, innate curiosity, and tenacity would be important to my skill set, I never knew how fast my fingers moved on my baby blue IBM Selectric would matter.

The test was held in the beautiful but crumbling old journalism building on the MSU campus, which would in the next couple of years be replaced with a gleaming new communication arts building. Everything in the old J school building was ancient, and we weren't provided with electric typewriters for the test but antique manual machines with spaces between each key wide enough to hold a ballpark frank. My shaking, sweaty fingers kept slipping off the keys, and at the end of the test, I had two long paragraphs of absolute gibberish. Three people taking the exam did not pass. One, an advertising major who had to pass the test at some point in her four-year college career shrugged, popped her gum, and flounced out. The other, another serious journalism hopeful, burst into tears and fled the room, and I've always wondered if she immediately changed her major to packaging or chicken science. I dragged myself down the steps of the ivy-covered building in disbelief before turning around to march back in and confront the TA with the unfairness of the situation.

"Do you want to repeat the test?" he asked wearily, taking in my tear-stained face.

"Yes, please?" I sobbed.

He handed me a slip of paper with a date and time and the room number in a less charming building in a newer part of campus.

When I arrived on the scheduled date, it was blessedly to a room filled with IBM Selectrics.

If I hadn't stood up for myself, I wouldn't have gone on to a career interviewing famous authors and politicians and covering boring city council meetings and a murder or two. I wouldn't have had a career I loved. And without the whole Oldsmobile summer job debacle, I never would have been brave enough to take a stand regarding the typing test.

Initially, I didn't mind the idea of working in the factory office. Dad took me in and introduced me around. It was crisp, clean-lined, and brightly lit. The staff—all women—wore pretty skirts and high heels. It seemed like an acceptable, if not thrilling, way to spend a summer.

"This is a very good job, you know. There are lots of people who spend their entire lives doing this work," Dad told me. It was probably the wrong thing for him to mention.

The summer between my sophomore and junior years, I had worked as a babysitter for the granddaughter of one of our neighbors on Cork Road. Mrs. Bristley always treated me with kindness, urging me to enjoy her homemade cookies and buying books of raffle tickets for the Morrice Homecoming. Win a TV! Win a steer! I would peddle them up and down Cork Road every summer. I adored her and was happy her son and his wife thought I was mature enough to take care of their only child—honestly, I probably wasn't.

My mother rose from her couch each morning at 6:30, throwing her barn coat over her pink or peach polyester shortie nightie and drove me in the 88 the mile and a half to the Bristley's mobile home.

Those sweltering days were all about the same. I'd sit on the couch and watch old black-and-white Westerns or Elvis Presley movies until my charge, a sweet, dark-haired little girl named Susie, woke up. I cleaned up the kitchen and washed the dinner dishes from the night before, vacuumed, dusted, and threw the laundry in the washing machine, then usually opened a can of Spaghettios for her lunch. By this time, I'd lost about twenty-five pounds by attending Weight Watchers classes with my friend, Becky, so my own lunch was usually cottage cheese, lettuce, and carrot sticks.

With all the newfound nutritional expertise I thought I had, I was worried I wasn't paying enough heed to Susie's health, so I forced the poor little kid to exercise by taking long nature walks in the blazing summer sun along the two-lane highway where the family lived. Occasionally, we ducked down under a small overpass for shade and to pick wildflowers, which in retrospect were just weeds. If anyone were interested in abducting a very naive fifteen-year-old and a cute little girl, I apparently wanted to make it as easy as possible for them. It's also amazing we didn't end up with poison ivy.

Working eight hours a day, five days a week, I earned seventy-five cents an hour and each Friday tucked my thirty dollars into my underwear drawer. At the end of summer, I took the bulk of my earnings to the bank in Morrice, where I deposited it for my future and kept fifty dollars to buy peasant blouses, painter pants, and Noxema.

I didn't have acne, but many of my friends did, and I desperately wanted my face to "belong to Noxema" as well. I also delighted in buying Gee, Your Hair Smells Terrific and Clairol Herbal Essence shampoo, ecstatic to leave my mother's urine-yellow, eye-stinging, astringent-smelling, watered-down Breck behind.

In the fall, both Susie and I went back to school, and I lost my job by default. Since I was thinner, I decided to give sports a chance. But the night before tryouts for basketball, my friend David called me to say the owner of the Morrice Restaurant—the only one in town—was looking for waitresses. David had told him about me.

"I don't have any experience," I said.

"Doesn't matter," David replied.

The lure of filthy lucre outweighed my desire to be on the team, so I went in for an interview and was hired on the spot. Mom took me to a local discount store and bought me one zip-up polyester tunic, a cross in color between mustard and a rotting banana, with a small white butterfly embroidered above the left breast. It was hideous, and I loved it. The entirety of my food service training entailed a sweet-faced sophomore named Karen who showed me around the place and reminded me to smile brightly at the customers to get the biggest tips.

"And . . . it wouldn't hurt if you unzipped your . . ." she hesitated, then gestured to my tunic, which was zipped up to my collarbone, "uh, *top* a tiny bit," she said.

I worked every Friday and Saturday night from 6:00 p.m. until 1:00 a.m. While older women took the breakfast and lunch shifts, the night waitresses—it would be years before the term "servers" gained traction—were all high school students. We took orders, poured beverages, made salads, worked the cash register, and sometimes washed the dishes ourselves, with absolutely no training. A more astute kid might have figured out a system for doing the job, but I wasn't the least bit astute. People yelled at me for never taking their orders or for letting their food sit under the warming lights too long.

"I've been looking at my soup and sandwich sitting up there for ten minutes!" a guy shouted, slamming his fist on the table and marching out.

I dumped a heaping plate of turkey, mashed potatoes, and gravy half into the lap of an old lady and half onto the mud-colored carpeting at her feet, then ran into the bathroom to cry, leaving Mark, the cook, to clean up my mess. Still, I wasn't fired.

Every two weeks, Jack, the owner, would stuff forty to fifty dollars into an envelope for me (I wouldn't learn the term "under the table" for many years), and each night, I toted home a huge bag of coins people had left for tips, likely because they were just polite or maybe because they knew my parents. All the money went into the underwear drawer to purchase my shampoo and face cream.

"Dear," a nice, forgiving man said as he got up from his table, wiping his mouth on his napkin and handing me a ten-dollar sympathy tip for a two-dollar bowl of soup, "you're a sweet kid. Promise me you won't do this for the rest of your life. Nobody deserves it. The *world* doesn't deserve it."

When I was done with work in the wee hours, I would call my father and wake him to come pick me up. I'd roil in my bed all night, smelling grease and hearing the restaurant noises.

I worked at the Morrice Restaurant for exactly six weeks. As much as I loved earning my $1.60 per hour minimum wage—more than double my pay for watching Susie—I hated everything about the job except my hideous tunic and the free diet soda.

"I want to quit," I told my mother, who didn't seem surprised. In such a small town, my lack of aptitude had likely gotten back to her by my second week on the job. Word spread fast in Morrice. We learned one old lady neighbor down Cork Road had phoned another old lady across the street to complain because even after I got my driver's license in November, I wasn't allowed to drive myself to work. Dad still got out of bed to pick me up.

"They're always spoiling that girl, I tell you," she reportedly said. "Like something could happen to her here, in Morrice."

"You can quit," my mother told me. "But you need to make the call yourself. This is your responsibility."

I called Jack, who also didn't seem surprised or disappointed, and then spoke with David the following Monday, thanking him for getting me the job and apologizing for leaving it so quickly.

"Not a problem," he said. "Jack just asked me if I knew any girls with big boobs, and I said yeah."

I didn't know whether to be insulted or flattered. Photos of me at the time show a teenager whose chest was barely more than concave.

After I graduated high school, my parents finagled a job interview for me at the bank where my cousin Kathy worked. I was just seventeen but personable, and Kathy thought I might be able to swing it as a teller. I was dismal at anything mathy, but I'd had that taste of earning money when I was in high school and definitely wanted more.

My interview at my cousin Kathy's bank the summer of 1977 was scheduled at the downtown Lansing headquarters. Being a relatively new driver, I'd never driven in a city bigger than Owosso, so I asked Mom if she would take me. My father changed his schedule to get home early and come along. I assumed they would either take a stroll along the shopping district or even wait in the car. But they both walked me into the building and took seats in the lobby.

I'm sure I completely flubbed the interview, embarrassed by knowing just outside the glass doors, visiting with the receptionist, my parents sat nervously waiting to hear how I had done. Obviously, I didn't get the job, and Kathy reported back the interviewer noted I was shy and subdued.

"Oh my God, Mother!" I wanted to scream. "Of course I was subdued! I was humiliated!"

Mom's parenting when I became a teenager was over-the-top, but ironically, when I was a younger child, it had seemed pretty laissez-faire.

Chapter 8

A FAILED TYPING TEST AND FOOD BY MR. HOT DOG

As a toddler, I slept in a closet-sized room at the top of the stairs in the old farmhouse. There were two larger, nicer rooms on the second level, but my parents probably chose it because it was the closest to their bedroom at the base of the first floor.

One of my earliest memories is awakening from an afternoon nap and calling for my mother, who didn't come. I shrieked for what seemed like hours. We were getting ready to move into the new house my parents were building just next door on a piece of property they had subdivided. I was about three and had been left home alone while Mom went to paint walls.

"You usually slept longer," she shrugged in later years when I reminded her of the abandonment. "I was right next door." But "next door" was one large pasture, one sizable garden plot, and one raspberry patch away.

Mom always giggled while relating the story of walking hand-in-hand with toddler me through Christian's

Department Store and me whispering to her that my under-pants were falling down.

"You began to shuffle your feet along like a little old man, and when I looked down, sure enough, there they were around your ankles," she'd laugh. "I told you just to step out of them, and I put them in my purse."

"And then we went home?"

She looked puzzled. "Then we finished shopping."

From the time I was old enough to force my chubby fingers to work buttons into holes, dressing myself was my responsibility. There weren't many photos of me from age three to six in a blouse with a hem that wasn't askew. Buttons and snaps were my nemesis. A macaw ate them off the back of my embroidered, sleeveless, cotton blouse while I posed, arms outstretched like a scarecrow with a huge colorful bird on each arm for a portrait at Busch Gardens in Florida.

"He's eating my buttons; he's eating my buttons; he's eating my buttons," six-year-old me whined frantically as Mom fiddled with her Brownie camera and told me to take my chin off my chest. It was glued there in a futile attempt to keep my top in place as it slid off my shoulders. I turned my unaccustomed Michigan eyes to the glaring Florida sun and tried to do as Mom said and smile brightly.

Taking decent photos was something that would elude Mom her entire life. Her poor subjects were unfailingly made to stand with perma-grins, arms awkwardly around each other, almost always squinting into the sun, as she commanded "a little to the right, wait, a little to the left, there we go, wait . . ." In her ninety-one years, she never once remembered to advance the film in a camera, and the entire process would begin again.

When she died, I took several yellow-and-red card-board Kodak cameras left scattered in her kitchen drawers to be developed. Not one had a photo we could put in an album without someone asking, "And . . . what is this?"

It's debatable whether her photography or driving skills were worse.

When I was four, I was allowed to ride in the front passenger seat; before getting too judgmental please remember seatbelts weren't mandatory in Michigan until 1985 and some pregnant women were still smoking ciggies and sousing down martinis when I was born.

One day while attempting to get out of a tight parallel parking spot in Owosso, Mom threw the 88 of the moment into reverse, jumped the curb, and backed into a huge old tree. I flew onto the floor of the car and the (obviously unreliable) patron saint of travelers, St. Christopher, lost his adhesive footing on the dashboard and conked me on the head. Luckily my frugal, Depression-era dad hadn't sprung for a more expensive saint and ours was a lightweight, made of cheap plastic.

Sometime in the late '70s, Dad decided to share rides to Oldsmobile with John Frye, the son of a good family friend, who had returned from serving in Vietnam and been hired at Olds. John was known as Young John, though I was never sure why since his father's name was Ed. During his stint in the service, we would go to the Fryes' farmhouse every few weeks and they would play a reel-to-reel recording of Young John's voice. Like many soldiers of the time, he sent recordings instead of letters to his parents. It seemed so modern.

On his first day of ride-sharing, Young John pulled up our dirt driveway and parked his sparkling new car by the row of tall cedars, which separated our gravel driveway from the garden. Later in the morning, forgetting about the carpool arrangement, Mom climbed into the 88, punched the button attached to the visor to operate our fancy new automatic door opener, winged out of the garage, swung the wheel dramatically to the right, smashed into Young John's beautiful new vehicle, and totaled it.

Our closest neighbor, Micky Shelest, heard the huge crash. When I say "neighbor," remember the Shelest home—which was the first home my parents owned, the one with the old maple tree—was at least an eighth of a mile away. The sound of the crash traveled across our driveway, through the cedar trees, across our garden and the field where we neighborhood kids played softball, soared over the raspberry patch, and Micky *still* heard it.

"It was so loud, I came out on the porch to see what in the world had happened," she told Dad later. "I saw Millie get out and look at her car, but then get back in and drive away, so I thought everything must be okay."

"There was nothing I could do." Mom shrugged. "And I had to go shopping."

"I thought Young John was going to cry," Dad said, describing the scene as the carpoolers pulled in the driveway. "He thought it was safe to leave his car in the *driveway*."

Obviously, her skills behind the wheel didn't improve with age because careening down a country road to Owosso one Sunday when she was well into her seventies, a sheriff's deputy pulled her over.

"Ma'am do you know why I stopped you?" "No, I most certainly do *not*, but I'm in a bit of a hurry," she said crisply, glancing pointedly down at her silver Timex.

"I'd say so," the exasperated cop exhaled. "Look, lady, you were going seventy-two in a fifty."

"I couldn't have been," Mom replied. "I'm on my way to church."

She was just that matter-of-fact during the McCaw eating my buttons incident. She simply put a bobby pin through the top holes on my blouse and twisted it tight and we continued our day, making sure to stop in at the Anheuser Busch Hospitality House so Dad could get a complimentary brew, which I'm sure he needed by then.

It was her MO again when, after meeting with a wedding photographer, Mom took Jim and me to Capitan's Restaurant in downtown Owosso for a sandwich. Some asshat had loosened the top of the mustard bottle on our table as a prank and poor, unknowing Jim gave it a hearty shake. One minute I was laughing at something someone said and the next everything in my field of vision was yellow. Mustard covered my bangs and face, and Jim had little globules hanging from his long eyelashes. There was stunned silence at the tables around us followed by muffled laughter. Jim and I were brilliant yellow, and Mom sat prim and pretty, completely untouched. We dashed to the restaurant bathroom to clean up as best we could, then slunk back to the table, too embarrassed to finish our meals.

"Mom, let's get out of here," I hissed.

"As soon as I'm done eating," she replied. She was nothing if not pragmatic.

Because both my parents wanted me to work at Oldsmobile the summer after my freshman year at college and I didn't want to disappoint them, I finally agreed to take the typing test. It was offered in an old Victorian home converted into offices in downtown Lansing within walking distance of my apartment and the *Lookout* offices, the Lansing Community College student newspaper where I worked as an editor my first two years of college before transferring to MSU.

Three times I trekked to the old house to take the test. Three times I failed miserably. It was embarrassing to call my mother and tell her the news after the first and second time. The third time was excruciating.

"You're kidding?" she asked.

"I am not. I'm so sorry. I tried my hardest, I promise."

"I don't believe you," she told me, after a long pause. "I think you *never* wanted to work at Oldsmobile at all and you failed the test on purpose."

I was shocked. I would not have done that, would I? It was true I wasn't too excited about an office job in a factory, especially after a recent trip to the Frandor Shopping Center in East Lansing when I saw an ad in the window for sales associates at a beautiful women's clothing store called Green's. I wasn't positive I would ever pass the typing test, and I absolutely needed to work. My parents gave me $100 a month throughout my college years and Social Security chipped in $167. I never really knew why I got Social Security because Mom initially said it had something to do with my adoption and later said it was because Dad had already retired, but I never questioned the reason because I needed the money. I was paid a small amount for working at the *Lookout* and had gotten some freelance writing work for a local ballet company. I was poor but still better off than most of my friends and certainly doing better than Jim, who resorted in his pre-veterinary student poverty to buying three-foot-long, yellow-waxed paper wrapped braunschweiger (liver sausage) for nineteen cents a pound. He ate the disgusting mush on cheap white bread with mustard. Sometimes, if he was more flush, he slapped a piece of processed cheese food on top of the mess.

Unable to work during the regular college semesters because of his intense schedule, he hired himself out to his uncle Walt's flywheel starter gear plant each summer. It was tough, demanding work, and he often had to toil on third shift with workers who disliked him because he was a college boy. He never told them he was also the owner's nephew because he thought it would make things even worse. The job paid well but he had to make the money he earned in three months last for twelve. I supported him by making him meals and buying him clothes whenever I could, so for a lot of reasons, I was motivated to earn some cash.

I walked through the sliding glass doors of Green's nervously, had an interview on the spot, and was hoping for a call and a job offer by the time I failed the third typing test. But I hadn't told my parents.

"You probably went into the test with that hangdog look you wear on your face," Mom said.

It would remain the most painful thing she ever said to me, and I hung up crying, my throat constricted, unable to defend myself.

Marilyn, the Kewpie-doll pretty, pixie-tressed petite blond manager of Green's, called soon after and offered me a job, which changed the trajectory of my life. I worked at each of the store's five locations throughout college and even after I graduated in 1982 while hunting for a newspaper job. I spent every Friday night, all day Saturday, and most of every Sunday teetering on foot-crippling Candie's brand mules—three-inch molded plastic heels with only a suede slide across my numb toes—sweet-talking frat boys into ordering monogrammed crew neck sweaters and button-down oxford shirts for their feathered-hair sorority girlfriends.

The college student staff worked "front of the store," selling Calvin Klein jeans and Lacoste jackets while the women over forty worked in "fine dresses," hawking Pendleton to Lansing's elite, including Earvin "Magic" Johnson's mother, who came in once a month or so and sent the saleswomen into a frenzy; we all got 30 percent off our purchases once we hit our quota in sales.

If the polite demeanor Millie instilled earned me a reputation as an ice princess among the more hard-nosed reporters at the MSU *State News*, where I covered the

International Student beat Sunday night through Thursday, it worked in my favor while selling expensive clothing. I met my quota every pay period.

My sales job gave me a lifelong appreciation of style, fashion, and creativity. Juggling the two jobs and a full credit load forced me to learn incredible time management skills. I considered it a bonus that, coming from small-town Morrice, I was also meeting fascinating people with personalities I'd never dreamed existed. Our immediate boss, Steve, would begin every big sales weekend and Black Friday event by sitting lotus style on the floor in the middle of the racks of silk and cashmere and meditating to bring the sales team good luck and high margins. Marilyn, who hired me, was only twenty-six but had already served in the military, had a young son, and was mature beyond her years. She was a fair, kind, and productive boss, and I liked her. Taking the job was not only the right decision and life altering—I knew I'd earned it completely on my own.

Still, the Oldsmobile argument remains the one fight I wish I never had with my mother, because all these years later, I'm still not sure she wasn't right. I know now I didn't want to work at Oldsmobile, yet I had no way of voicing it to my parents without seeming ungrateful.

We had a painting of an early model Oldsmobile in our living room and served our iced tea out of pitcher with the Olds logo imprinted on the side. The Catholic Church, his family, and Oldsmobile were the focal points of my father's life. But it was Dad's world, and I wanted to create one of my own. I wanted to break free of the constraints of my parents and what felt like an entire town knowing my every move. I wanted to grow up.

Painful as the Great Typing Test Incident of 1978 was, if I hadn't realized my mother thought I came across so miserably, I might not have walked back up those steps of the ivy-covered journalism building the next year and demanded another shot at my dream.

My only other fights with Mom were regarding our wedding—not my marriage to Jim, who both my parents adored, but our wedding. Mom didn't care for one of my bridesmaids, a young woman who had been a wonderful friend when we were children but who had a traumatic childhood. She had essentially ignored me once we hit ninth grade, and many years later placed the blame on me for our lost friendship. But I'd included her for sentimental reasons. I still believed in the kind, funny, and supportive child she had once been and wanted desperately to latch on to the good memories.

"Let it go, *please*, Mom," I said. And for some reason, she did.

"Mr. Hot Dog" was another point of contention. Sitting down and talking with our parents when we announced our engagement, we all developed a financial plan: Mom and Dad would pay for the reception venue—my father's Knights of Columbus Hall in Owosso, nothing else was even considered—the food, and the flowers, while Jim's parents would cover the rehearsal dinner and the alcohol at the reception. Jim and I would take care of our clothing, honeymoon, and the gifts for our bridesmaids and groomsmen.

The process went as seamlessly as possible. Mom never complained when I simply chose the pattern for my dress without inviting her along or even asking her advice.

When my daughter Molly got married in 2017, I attended each of her bridal salon appointments. We had lunches and brunches and overnight trips to visit boutiques around the state, and it was a precious, poignant part of the wedding process. I would have been devastated if I wasn't included.

But for my own wedding, I went by myself to find a pattern and material at a fabric store located in Frandor on my lunch hour from Green's one Saturday, then hired the seamstress at the store to make my dress. I showed Mom the pattern as an afterthought, along with a swatch of the heavy, creamy, satin material I was considering. She loved the pattern but balked at the material.

"Doesn't it come in white?" she asked.

Her implication was clear. My independent and spirited mother, always described as a woman before her time, was still a woman who'd been born in 1916. In her world, when you got married, you wore white. Unless you were one of *those* girls.

Which, of course, I was. I'd willingly rushed to give up my virginity at sixteen, a fact I'm pretty sure my mother had surmised and accepted, but which she certainly didn't want to advertise.

"That's so old-fashioned, Mom," I bristled. "Besides, I look better in cream."

"Actually, you look better in white," she sniffed.

We had a rare shouting match then, which ended, as usual, with me in tears and her turning on her heel and walking away, a stubborn set to her chin.

I went to the store the same day and angrily bought the white satin.

The next morning, she came as close to apologizing to me as she ever would when I called to tell her she had won.

"I want you to know," she said, a catch in her throat, "I didn't sleep last night."

A few years later, when it was popular to have your "colors" done, the annoyingly cheerful consultant draping swaths of sateen material around my neck told me I should never, under any circumstances, wear cream.

"You should always, always wear white! It will look so much nicer on you! Cream will wash you right out!" she exclaimed. I shouldn't have been surprised.

Dress drama behind us, we turned to the food selection.

All of the weddings I'd attended growing up followed a similar pattern—an afternoon or evening ceremony in a Protestant or Catholic church followed immediately by a sedate reception with cake and coffee in a church basement or a raucous blowout at a town community center or VFW hall. Someone either played records or there might be a country western band.

A month after I got married, my maid-of-honor Meg, a friend and coworker from Green's who had grown up in a wealthy Detroit suburb, got married and her reception was held in a beautiful hotel ballroom. It was a sit-down affair with a tuxedoed group of musicians playing standards. It was the first time I realized there *was* a different sort of wedding and reception.

But in planning our own, and since I didn't yet know any other type of wedding fare existed, I had no objection to a buffet. I *did*, however, have an objection—a very big one—to having the food catered by "Mr. Hot Dog."

"Mom, no!" I begged. "There has just *got* to be some-place else."

"The food is very good," she said. "We've been to several receptions where they have used them, and people just love it."

She dragged Jim and I down to the restaurant, a sort of homegrown KFC, and ordered a chicken, mashed potatoes, and vegetable sampler plate. For summertime, homestyle, picnic-type food, big platters of chicken, and heaping bowls of coleslaw, Mr. Dog fare worked out just fine.

And, once again, Millie was right.

Chapter 9

PURGATORY VS. CHURCH
OF THE LAST RESORT

Mrs. Eddington is of the Protestant Faith and attends church at St. Johns in Owosso. Mr Eddington is of the Catholic Faith and attends St. Mary's Church in Morrice, Michigan.

Mr. and Mrs. Eddington were married February 9th, 1946. Their marriage has been a happy one and religion has presented no problem to them. They have not, as yet, decided where Patty will attend church as she grows older. At the present time she goes with her mother to St. Johns Church. They do not feel that the religious question will ever be a problem for them.

—Taken directly from the Report of Investigation re: Patricia Ann Eddington, (Mary Ann Ball), April 2, 1962. File No. 693— (Mrs. Barbara Trezise, Court Worker)

My parents were married on one of those frigid February days in Michigan that make your lips stick to your teeth and your lungs ache if you breathe too deeply. They took their solemn vows at the side altar of Epiphany Parish in Detroit. Even though Dad's uncle—the same priest Dad lived with in Adrian while he was in high school—offici-ated, they could not be married at the front of the church because my mother was not Catholic. Even though their *mixed marriage* would ultimately lead to many delays as they tried to adopt a child—Catholic Social Services refused to help them unless Mom would convert—the "mix" never seemed to affect them.

"We never fought once over religion," my mother told me. "We couldn't understand why people would argue over something so silly."

She happily used their different faiths to shoo away the Jehovah Witness folk who pulled up to the Cork Road house once a year or so, the crunch of their car wheels on the gravel driveway giving Mom advance notice unexpected visitors were on the way.

"We have *three* people and two religions in this house already," she'd tell them sweetly. "Do *you* think we need one more?"

She was just as disarming when the Hoover salesmen or Avon ladies came calling and feared coming up our steps to the front porch where my gentle but lumbering and large mutt Queenie lay in her usual spot, just to the left of the screen door.

"Does he bite?" they'd ask, tentatively.

"Only if I *tell her* to," she'd reply.

Honestly, the single time I remember either of my folks becoming edgy on the religion topic was my fault. Informed by my Catholic neighbor and playmate Patty about the con-cept of purgatory when we were seven, I told her she was a dirty rotten liar, then ran home to tattle to my folks.

"Don't *you* ever question something simply because *you* haven't heard of it." Dad pointed his forefinger at my ashen face as I nodded. It was so rare for him to raise his

voice to me, I never forgot the abject shame I felt. Ironically, one of the only other times I recalled him shouting at
me was more than thirty years later as I prepared to host a
fiftieth anniversary party for my parents in the St. Mary's
Catholic Church parish hall in Morrice. Dashing around
to find where the Styrofoam cups, napkins, and sugar and
creamer packets were, I stubbornly ignored his admonition
to wait for the ladies from the guild, who would be serving
the cake and beverages, and tried to start the hulking stain-
less steel Bunn coffee maker myself.

"Don't *you* touch that!" he yelled.

There was that "you" again. What he was likely saying
those times was, "Don't *you*, little know-it-all, claim there
is no purgatory" and "Don't *you*, officious daughter of
mine, take away a job those guild members are actually
looking forward to doing." But what I *heard* was, "Don't
you . . . you *non-Catholic . . .*"

As a child, I *wanted* to be Catholic. Had the topic
ever *really* been up for discussion—I don't think they
hadn't "yet decided where Patty will attend church when
she grows older"—I would have begged for the right to
walk into St. Mary's with my father, dip my fingers in the
holy water font, and kneel reverently on the bench with my
forehead bowed to my clasped hands.

When I was about six, I'd attended a candlelit wedding on a winter night at St. Mary's, and it was beauty and
majesty. During the reception at the Morrice Community
Center afterward, I stood on top of my father's size 13,
shiny Florsheim shoes as he waltzed me across the floor,
and I felt pure joy.

My mother and I belonged to United Church of
Christ—a denomination I later came to call The Church of
the Last Resort because we welcomed human beings other
religions sometimes condemned. Being Protestant meant

being hugged to the sizable bosoms of elderly German immigrants attending coffee hour after service each Sunday. It also meant being forced to go to sauerkraut suppers and slide show travelogues, where church members showed off their trips to Austria and Switzerland. I'd come to learn as I grew that the liberal UCC—the first mainline Christian church to support same-sex marriage—was *exactly* the place for someone with my belief system. But as a kid, I wanted the chanting, incense, silk robes, and ceremony of my father's religion.

Dad's faith was staunch. He attended Mass every Sunday, even when we were traveling out west to see his aunt Nina and uncle Fred or to Florida to see Mom's brother, my uncle Bill, and his family. We'd pull into a motel in Phoenix or Santa Fe or Pompano Beach on a Saturday night. Dad would first lug in our suitcases and Mom's blue-and-tan Samsonite train case, which held her makeup and medicines, then look for the nearest church in the phone book always placed in the bedside drawer. He'd rise quietly the next morning, and often by the time Mom and I were up and dressed and ready to head out for eggs or oatmeal, he'd already be back telling us about the beauty of the stained-glass windows or the majesty of the altar at the new church he'd visited.

Once, driving through Albuquerque, he gasped and yelled, "Goddammit, Millie! Yesterday was *Friday*!" It was spring break and therefore Lent. Dad had forgotten and ordered a hamburger and milkshake the night before, and during Lent, he only ate fish or waffles or pancakes for Friday night dinner. On the rare occasions we were home during Lent, we inevitably drove the two miles to the intersection of Morrice and Lansing roads to an ancient and rambling roadhouse restaurant called The Longhorn Steakhouse. They had an excellent fish fry dinner on Friday nights, but I didn't like fish then. He always ordered me a hamburger basket with extra pickles and chocolate milk. I was a huge fan of Lent.

I'm sure Dad told the priest about his hamburger transgression at his next confession, which he also never missed. My father's beliefs were so firm and based in fairness, he never attended confession in Morrice where the priest would undoubtedly recognize his voice and his stutter. He thought he might not get the fair amount of penance. He'd go instead to various churches in Owosso or Lansing to confess his sins.

"I've never understood why your father even *goes* to confession," my mother's youngest sister, Dorothy, would say. "I've never seen him do *anything* he'd need to confess."

In fairness, Aunt Dorothy lived seventy-five miles away and wasn't around to hear all those "goddammit, Millie!" episodes.

The fire of my passion over Dad's Catholicism was stoked even further because I actually *knew* God's wife—or at least one of them—my great-aunt, Sister Rosina.

The sister of my father's mother, Mary, she was born Agnes Jordan but became a novice of the Immaculate Heart of Mary (IHM) order at seventeen or eighteen and was known ever after as Rosina. She worked as a piano teacher at Marygrove College in Detroit, but by the time I remember her, she was already living at the IHM motherhouse in Monroe. It was an almost three-hour trip from Morrice, but from early childhood through my senior year in high school, my little family made the trek at least once every five or six weeks. In the summer, we packed picnic lunches of turkey and ham sandwiches and potato salad and big jugs of iced tea and ate in the beautiful gardens tended by the IHM sisters garbed in their full, heavy habits with long veils. Each Christmas Eve afternoon, we paraded through the brick-walled halls with their arched doorways from Sister Rosina's room in the infirmary to the cathedral. There, we listened with reverence as the sisters in the choir practiced hymns for midnight mass.

To my young eyes, it was all so gorgeous, otherworldly, ethereal, and reminiscent of *The Sound of Music*. I told my father I thought Catholic people must be the most religious people of *all* religious people and mused I might also like to be a nun.

"I wonder how hard it would be?"

His eyes crinkled but he didn't laugh.

"Well, Buddy, I think first you might have to be Catholic."

As if *that* had been up to me.

I couldn't sit quietly for twenty minutes while Mom "spit set" my hair during Lawrence Welk on Saturday night, but I never complained about those long car trips to see my great-aunt. I thought it was sad we could never take Sister Rosina gifts for her birthday or holidays—at least nothing she could keep.

In the 1960s, IHM nuns were asked to share whatever little tokens they received with their fellow sisters. Monetary gifts were put into a fund, and they could make requests for small amounts of cash to purchase trinkets from the infirmary canteen.

They were also not allowed to stay overnight at the homes of relatives, a rule which affected our family in a very sad way in July 1966.

Looking back, so much of my life was colored by the horrible events of that summer, leaving me with a fear of imminent danger I've struggled to shake my entire life.

I'd been lying on my stomach watching television before bed when the phone rang.

I don't remember what show was on, but I remember the anxiety I felt listening to my mother's shaking voice during the conversation. I kept my eyes fixed firmly to the TV and pretended not to listen so my parents wouldn't send me from the room. I could tell something *big* had happened. Mom hung up and had a whispered conversation with Dad in the kitchen, then returned to the phone where she made several calls asking friends if I could stay with them. No one was available, so my parents took me to the funeral of a young woman killed in one of the most horrific mass murders of modern times.

After talking with Mom, Dad came back into the living room and sunk into his La-Z-Boy, but he didn't recline. He sat stiffly, staring blankly ahead, both hands resting quietly on his knees. Even at such a tender age, I could tell I shouldn't ask what had happened, and I wouldn't truly understand what occurred until several years later.

Mary Ann Jordan, the daughter of Dad's cousin Phil Jordan, was one of eight young women slaughtered in a Chicago nursing school townhouse by a drifter and some-time cargo boat worker named Richard Speck. It was a horrific crime, which captured the nation's attention and broke the collective heart of my father's family. Mary Ann did not even live at the townhouse where the murder occurred but was spending the night with her brother Phil Jr.'s fiancée, Suzanne Farris, so they could discuss plans for the upcoming wedding.

"Young Phil lost both his sister *and* his fiancée that horrible night," my parents would always say, shaking their heads sadly when they discussed the murders.

I remember the huge cathedral where the funeral was held and emerging out into the hot summer sunshine, where crowds of onlookers and photographers clicked photos of the mourners. A picture of my father and my uncle Frank appeared in a group shot at the cemetery in one of the major news magazines of the time, *Life* or *Look*, I don't remember which. My mother kept the publication high on a shelf in a closet as a grim reminder of the tragedy. I unearthed it while helping her and Dad pack to leave Cork Road and move to a smaller home in 1996.

"Throw it away," Mom said, sadly. "I don't even know why I kept it."

We made the trip to Chicago with Uncle Frank and my father's sister Liz but—at a time she probably longed to be with us—without Sister Rosina. Another IHM nun had accompanied her to the city, and she'd had to grieve the loss of her great-niece not with her family but in a convent nearby.

A couple years later we were allowed to take her on a day trip to Illinois to see her nephew Phil—Mary Ann's father—and his wife and remaining children. The ride home was the first car trip I'd seen Uncle Frank—normally given to singing funny songs and chatting about stories he'd seen on the news—subdued. Sitting between him and Sister Rosina in the back seat, I noticed her head begin drooping and then she began softly snoring.

"Oh, no!" she jolted up a little bit later, mortified. "I'm so sorry; I didn't mean to fall asleep!"

"Aunt Agnes," Dad, our driver, said kindly. "It was a long day and a hard, emotional visit. You needed to rest a bit. Shucks, I slept for about forty-five minutes a little while ago myself."

Her face froze and then she burst into the sweetest laughter.

"Oh, Jimmy," she said. "You behave now, you rascal."

Cleaning out old boxes one day, Molly found an essay I'd written about Sister Rosina, which was printed in the *Detroit Free Press Sunday Magazine* in the early 1980s. I'd written about how she watched for us when she knew we were going to visit, sitting in her chair by the window, and how we'd eventually been allowed to bring her little gifts she loved like Jordan Almonds, for her surname, and Blue Nun wine. I drove to Monroe the next morning with a copy of the magazine as a surprise. But another nun had already seen the piece and alerted her.

She was standing in the hallway outside the door of her room, grinning, after the front desk called to alert her to my arrival.

"I didn't want you to find me sitting in my chair by the window," she laughed.

Not long after, I made the trip to Monroe by myself again.

"She's not doing well," Mom said on one of our daily phone calls. "You might want to go."

She was waiting—not by the door and not in her chair—in bed. Weak and frail, she held my hand and asked if I thought she would be in very much pain at the end of her life.

This woman, who had given herself to God as a teenager and who I had assumed viewed death as a *promotion* was still afraid of dying. It reinforced for me what I began to understand when Mary Ann was killed—for all its beauty and wonder, the world can still at times be a terrifying place. I gathered myself and kissed her cheek.

"I hope not. I really hope not," I told her. "Not if there is any mercy."

And I realized that, sauerkraut-eating Protestant or holy water–dipping Catholic nun, *nobody* is exempt from fear.

Chapter 10

APPLICATION TO
ADOPT A CHILD

Following their small wedding, Dad tripped on the slippery steps while carrying his groom's cake into the church basement reception hall, folding it neatly in half and smearing himself with chocolate frosting and thus forging the "funny wedding story" he would drag out for his entire life. After their marriage, my folks settled into a cozy flat in the upstairs of a downtown Detroit brownstone. Mom attended beauty school and Dad went to work at a body shop owned by a friend. They began planning a family and almost immediately started a fund for "Junior."

I'm not sure how long they tried and hoped and dreamed. But ultimately the troublesome, painful menstrual cycles, which plagued Mom for years, forcing her to bed three or four days a month, led to a hysterectomy.

They moved to the country in 1950—amidst those dire warnings from Mom's mother—and on October 15, 1957, submitted an Application to Adopt a Child in Shiawassee County. It was completed by my mother, in pencil.

GENERAL INFORMATION

Surname of Family: Eddington

Date: October 15, 1957

Father's Name: James Eddington

Birthplace: Morrice

Address: 9130 Cork Road

Birthdate: January 18, 1919

Nationality: Irish

Occupation: Factory and Farm

Age: 37

Telephone: Morrice 64F3

Income: $5,000

Religion: Catholic

Education: Grad high school

Were you previously married? No

Date of Present Marriage: February 9, 1946

Where Married: Epiphany Church, Detroit

Mother's Maiden Name: Mildred Block

Birthplace: Detroit

Age: 40

Education: Grad high school

Birthdate: July 11, 1916

Religion: Protestant

Occupation: Housewife

Church Affiliation: St. John's, Owosso

Were you previously married? No

Nationality: German

Number of Children in Home: 0

Sex and Age of Child Wanted: Under 4 years; either sex

HOME

Date Purchased: January 1, 1949
Cost: $8,000
Balance Due: $4,300
Payment per Month: $50
Number of Rooms: 8

REMARKS

We live in this place, and it is a farm with 150 acres. Have been out here for about six years.

Several notations were scrawled in ink in the margins across the Application to Adopt a Child by a court worker.

"Impossible to have own children, willing to pay med and hospital bills."

"4/10/58 stopped in."

"2/25/59 will take up to five years."

Then the largest note, underlined,

"Child placed in home 7/7/61."

I was the child.

I wonder if my parents sat down one night and discussed the parameters of their application or if they did it over Dad's pancakes on a Sunday morning? Did they negotiate, one of them wanting a boy, one of them saying, "Maybe we should consider an older child?" My softhearted father wasn't the best negotiator.

For years he would go out each night to hook Queenie to the chain at her doghouse, then come back into the living room and stand in front of Mom, who'd be watching TV. "What do you think, Millie? Should Queenie have a graham cracker?"

It was the same scenario every night. Mom always seemed to consider his question carefully, then each time she would incline her head and nod slightly. Dad always looked relieved, then went to the kitchen and got the dog *two* graham crackers.

I came to realize it wasn't that Mom held the power in the "should-the-dog-get-a-bedtime-snack" part of their relationship, but they had a true partnership and discussed even the smallest and most trivial of matters. They were married for sixty-one years, so it obviously worked. They negotiated many more important issues than the Queenie/ graham cracker question during those six decades—whether to buy a cottage, when I should be allowed to date, if Dad should run for school board again, and if it was time for him to retire from Oldsmobile.

I can only imagine their conversation, but because they were deliberate, thoughtful people, I assume they talked at length about the type of child they hoped to adopt. They had obviously expanded their parameters of what type of child they would take when nothing happened in the months after the application was filed. One of them, I assume it was Mom, then stopped in at the probate court office in April of 1958 to say they would take a child of "up to five years."

They probably never dreamed it would take so long. Despite their apparent willingness to be flexible, their dream of having a child would ultimately drag on for nearly eighteen years after their wedding day.

Someone must have convinced Mom and Dad the road to adoption led through the tangled and frustrating foster care system, because in the mid-1950s, they began taking in a steady stream of youngsters. A brother and a sister named Butch and Esther stayed awhile and seemed to be among my parents' favorites from the stories they later told me. But the kids' mother discovered their whereabouts, came to the farmhouse drunk, and screamed profanities on the front lawn in the middle of the night, and ultimately the court moved them. There were a few other foster children and then came their great hope . . . Timmy.

Timmy was a beautiful cherub with blond curls and an enchanting grin, and my parents tried desperately to adopt him.

Whenever I tell the story of the first memory in my life, which includes Timmy, people say, "But you can't possibly remember it. You were just a toddler." I question it, too, but the scene is so absolutely vivid to me. I am reaching up to hold the hand of a woman who wears a white glove, remember it was the early 1960s and gloves for daywear were the norm. We are walking across the cement porch of the farmhouse. Framed in the doorway are a tall man, a petite blond woman, and a small boy. They are all smiling, the little boy peeking shyly out from behind the woman's dress.

Was the woman with me the court caseworker named Mrs. Day, whom Mom talked about fondly through the years? Had Mrs. Day told me something good was going to happen? Whatever the truth is about the little tableau, what I remember most is the *feeling*. "Welcome," the family seemed to be saying. "Welcome."

While I was a student at MSU, I wrote an article about adoption for a magazine writing class. I interviewed the sister of one of my classmates, who had just brought home a little girl. Visiting with the young mother in her lovely, comfortable home, she confessed when I had called her and began the conversation with, "You don't know me but . . ."

she was immediately terrified, thinking I was her daughter's birth mother and had tracked her down.

I'd think of the conversation with more empathy decades later when my eyelash lady, Jackie, made her "Oh, I get it. You were in disguise" comment.

I also interviewed a psychologist for the article. While I can't recall anything else she told me and the article has long since disintegrated in a landfill, I do recall what she said when I mentioned my first memory about my parents with Timmy and that I was worried it took place only in my imagination.

"Actually, it's totally possible you remember it," she told me. "Even if it turned out happily, at the time it was a very traumatic event for you. Even the youngest of children can remember a traumatic event."

But mostly, the stories I have about Timmy are ones I heard from my parents, and there are many . . . so many I spent a lot of years being jealous of the little boy.

"He was such a cute little bugger," my father would say, then tell the story again of how Timmy, who was deaf, once accompanied him to the "big" barn—our farm also had a smaller hip roof barn, a corn crib, a granary, and the tiny gas house where Dad filled the orange metal can every time I almost ran out of gas. Intent on his chores, Dad lost track of Timmy for a moment, and when he remembered he'd better check on him, he saw Timmy above him running along the beams.

"I yelled and motioned for him to go back to the hayloft and come down the ladder," Dad said, laughing, his eyes watering as he remembered the scene. "And the little bugger just smiled and reached up and turned off his hearing aid."

My mother worked tirelessly to make sure Timmy got the best of everything he needed, drove across state to make sure he had the finest of hearing aids, and investigated how to learn sign language or lip reading. I can imagine the joy as my parents stood in their doorway with the little boy they hoped would be their son as the little girl they hoped would be their daughter walked toward them.

I was placed in my parents' home in July 1961, and I remember visiting Santa with Timmy, so my folks must have had at least five months of feeling like a complete family. There was never any long discussion about what happened to him. I was told his mother also proved problematic, and the probate court decided he would be better off living farther away. He was adopted by a family in Ohio, professors who were both hearing impaired, according to Mom and Dad. Their sadness at the loss was never discussed, and I eventually understood how deep it was through what they didn't say as what they always did: "He was such a cute little bugger."

Chapter 11

HULA-HOOP QUEEN

....

Financial status: Mr. and Mrs. Eddington own their farm house and surrounding acres with no mortgage. They have a new Oldsmobile, which is paid for. They have no outstanding debts.

—Taken directly from the Report of Investigation re: Patricia Ann Eddington, (Mary Ann Ball), April 2, 1962. File No. 693— (Mrs. Barbara Trezise, Court Worker)

....

Growing up, I assumed our little family was rich, so I was surprised when as an adult I learned of my parents' modest income. Mom hadn't worked outside the home since their marriage, and she confided in me once that at the height of his earning powers Dad had never made more than $18,000 a year at Oldsmobile. While $18,000 was a huge increase from the $5,000 noted in their 1956 Application to Adopt, it was still below the $21,063 average household income in the United States in 1980 when he retired. Living without debt, never having a credit card until they took a trip to Hawaii for their fortieth anniversary in 1986 and needed one to rent a car, they managed to live a beautiful and very comfortable life.

I have early sepia-toned memories of walking behind Mom as she hauled pots, pans, and kitchen utensils in my little red wagon from the old farmhouse to the new redbrick ranch next door. Designed with a mid-century, minimalist flair, the house eventually had a Quasar TV and the first Amana Radarange (a microwave) we'd ever seen. We also had our cottage at Town Line Lake, and I had a new-to-me Evinrude snowmobile so I could ride along the trails at the lake behind my father's new, shiny, red Bolens Husky machine.

That Dad had a snowmobile was a testament to his quiet brilliance. At Oldsmobile they had a suggestion program, and Dad and one of his coworkers submitted an idea, which somehow eliminated one nut and one bolt in some part of a car's construction. I was young and didn't really understand or care what the idea was.

What I *do* remember is Dad coming home late from work one night, which was unheard of. He'd stopped at a snowmobile dealer in a nearby town and purchased the Husky with a portion of the few-thousand-dollar bonus he'd received for his idea. He did it even before telling Mom of the windfall; I'm not sure why—she would never have criticized the decision. It was the only time I ever heard of my father treating himself to something or acting spontaneously in his entire life.

The thought is both heartbreaking and heartening.

Otherwise, my parents lived in their lovely home in a frugal way. My mother canned vegetables and made strawberry and raspberry freezer jam and a very mild homemade chili sauce, which Dad always said was so spicy it made his bald head sweat. I carried my bologna sandwich, apple, and homemade chocolate chip cookie to school in a yellow, plastic Yogi Bear lunch box, which always smelled vaguely of mustard instead of spending forty-five cents a day on hot lunch. I was allowed two cents a day for a carton of milk. I stashed the weekly dime away. When we went into town so Mom could get a hunk of cheese from the big wheel of cheddar at Hathaway's Grocery Store, I used my money to buy chocolate ice cubes and wax bottle candies. Mom used a suds saver, which allowed her to reuse washing machine water and detergent. Our laundry was hung on a clothesline from April to October, and my school clothes were exchanged every afternoon for playclothes so they could be worn several times.

o o o

Every weekday had an assigned purpose: Mondays were for laundry; Tuesdays for ironing; Wednesdays for grocery shopping; Thursdays covered a hodgepodge of leftover chores, like mowing our huge lawn on our big, green, John Deere lawnmower, working in the garden, and attending meetings of her Morrice Women's Club or St. John's UCC Church Guild; and Fridays were for vacuuming and dusting.

She wasn't always home by the time I returned from school at 3:00 p.m., so I was instructed to wait on the front porch since she didn't think I was responsible enough for a key. She was probably correct, and it's a testament to the safety of our town that she trusted my fate more to being left alone outside as an eight-year-old than to being allowed entrance to the house. More than once I waited so long I had to rush to the protection of the center of the corn crib walls and pull down my stirrup pants to urinate on the hard earth. I still have an unreasonable fear of not being able to take a pee when necessary.

Saturday nights were reserved for a soak in the tub with my "Crazy Foam" dispensed from a metal clown can. After my bath, Mom would have me sit on the tall telephone seat with the atomic starburst design, which she'd move into the living room. We would watch *The Lawrence Welk Show* as she spit set my hair with pink foam rollers in preparation for church Sunday. I'd already had a shampoo in the basement laundry sink with her favorite diluted Breck, my eyes protected from the strong, astringent smell with a blue, plastic, pleated hair shield, which looked like a flying saucer, tucked above my ears.

The night before my junior prom, after decorating the high school gym with crepe paper and balloons all day, I hesitantly asked Mom if it might be okay if I washed my hair Saturday afternoon instead, since I would be missing the evening ritual and it would smell fresh for the big dance. The look of first surprise then sadness on her face meant, I believe, she didn't realize I still felt I had to ask her permission. But she'd never told me it was okay to leave the old childhood rules behind, and I'd never asked; not because I was afraid but because I still never wanted to do or say anything to make my parents think I was unhappy in any way.

Many of my cousins later confessed they'd been concerned about me when I was a kid because I'd gotten over the outgoing phase the court worker had described and became meek, shy, and unable to maintain eye contact. They thought as I matured, I'd either sink my nose further into my books or rebel like a maniac and shoot up smack or hustle on the corner.

Mom and Dad—mostly Mom, probably—*did* want me to have good manners. From an early age I was expected to walk tall, sit straight, not interrupt, get my elbows off the table, and above all never be "sassy." Being sassy was the ultimate misdemeanor and always earned me twenty minutes in my room reading *My Big Book of Manners*, where a group of teddy bears, giraffes, and an elephant were invited to a birthday party and demonstrated the benefits of being polite.

"We could always take you anywhere; you were so well-behaved," Mom told me. Until I was nearing middle age and Mom "softened" in the opinion of my cousins, compliments on my manners were among the only types she would offer so I didn't become big-headed.

"My goodness, Patti turned out to be just beautiful," one of Mom's friends whispered in apparent and insulting surprise as they sat in a tent waiting for the cakewalk to start at the Homecoming, an annual summer carnival hosted by the Lions Club.

"Shh," Mom said, sotto voce. We don't want her to turn out vain."

I was twenty-two and already married at the time.

Throughout childhood, I was a pet to most adults, but my peers took a look at my sway back and protruding stomach, my unusually large teeth and big feet, and picked me second to last in almost every game of kickball, coming in just before a slight boy with a lisp.

There was only one quasi-athletic thing I could do well: Hula-Hoop. Mom purchased a hot pink hoop for me at Murphy's 5&10 in Owosso the winter before, likely hoping it would help me reduce my chubby midsection. It didn't, but it did become my most prized possession, and I became such an adept and voracious twirler, the household quickly had strict rules about just where and how often I was allowed to walk around with my sand-filled, noisy, spinning hoop. After a close call with a vintage lamp during a babysitter's watch, the Hula-Hoop rule was "as often as you want but *never* inside." I was tireless and became so skilled I could raise and lower the hoop from my neck past my belly down to my ankles and back up again. I could circle it on my wrist for minutes at a time.

"Look at that little bugger go," my dad would say.

In the summer of 1968, Perry held a diamond jubilee celebration to celebrate their seventy-five-year history as a city. Men grew beards or risked being fined for charity, and women dressed in bustles and carried parasols. Commemorative wooden nickels were distributed, and an unlikely Hula-Hoop contest was advertised in the newspaper. Even though I was only in third grade, I was a voracious reader. My parents were both news hounds, and they inspired the love in me. This led to lots of meaningful questions like, "Where is Vietnam?" Some questions were uncomfortable, though, like the time I yelled across a beauty salon "What is rape?" while reading a magazine as Mom got a perm.

Sadly, the Hula-Hoop competition was based solely on stamina, not on the ability to perform any of the tricks I'd mastered, but I was still confident of a win.

"I'm going to be the Hula-Hoop *queen*," I told my folks.

"It's not that kind of contest, Buddy," my father said.

Every summer that *wasn't* the Perry sesquicentennial, we local kids saved our twenty-five-cent allowances, dimes from the tooth fairy, and two-dollar birthday gifts from relatives for our annual summer carnival, the Morrice Homecoming.

Sponsored by the Lions Club as a fundraiser for Leader Dog for the Blind, the three-day event was a cacophony of the aforementioned cakewalks, carnival rides, and games. A big amusement company from Ohio brought in rides like the Tilt-A-Whirl and the Scrambler and scattered them over the high school football field. Lions' members covered the neighboring tennis courts with food tents and games like Roll-A-Score. Contestants rolled a rubber ball down a shoot to numbered cubbyholes, and if they rolled under twelve or over twenty-nine points, they won a stuffed animal.

A charter member of the Lions, my father not only built Roll-A-Score, he housed the game in our barn the other 362 days a year and traveled to a big warehouse in Lansing to pick up huge clear, plastic bags of fiber-filled purple bears and lime-green giraffes for prizes. He piled the bags up along the wall in our garage until Homecoming weekend. I snuck out to see them at night and bragged about it to my friends. It was heady stuff being Dad's kid.

The best thing about the Homecoming was it didn't come with the seedy underbelly feel of some of the fairs and festivals Mom and Dad liked to drag me through. One year there was a tent with oddities featuring a dead piglet born with two heads. It made me cry, but that's about as macabre as the event ever got.

Dad spent the entire weekend down at the site, snacking on the sandwiches and slurping the iced tea Mom would bring him or occasionally grabbing a hot dog and 7-Up from the food tent. Years later, I learned it was not all he was doing. A high school classmate messaged me once when I posted something about the Homecoming on Facebook. Her father, a local insurance agent, was in a wheelchair and loved to go to the event to visit with his friends.

"We weren't strong enough to push our dad in the wheelchair through the grass," she told me. "Your dad would see us arrive and always come to assist my dad to the tennis court so he could get to the games and talk with people."

And a woman whose husband was in the Lions Club surprised me by telling me my father, who I never thought of as very progressive, actually was, even if by default. He always tried to do what was right.

"Back in those days, the men/fathers would not work in the PTO food booth except to set up and take down," she said. "But your dad and Dick [her husband] did. They were the first two I remember who would."

It was a small town in a time when women were still called housewives, and there was a big divide between the roles of the moms and dads I knew. But Dad and Dick didn't care. They worked selling hot dogs and soda beside the women. They were obviously the trailblazers because by the time I was old enough to attend the festivities, there were lots of men working in the booth.

I saw any moment not spent at the Homecoming as a waste of precious time and resented it each afternoon when Mom told me it was time to go home, get out of the blazing July sun, and rest for a couple of hours. After minutes of her nagging and my whining, we'd eventually find the 88 on the dusty field where we'd parked and head home. She'd flop on the couch, put her feet up, and try to ignore my constant "When are we going *back*? When are we going back?" nagging. I'm sure it wasn't restful. She probably wished she'd just stayed in town.

In addition to the rides and games, the Homecoming always featured wonderful cakewalks every few hours with a pleasant-faced old Lion named Merlin Doyne shouting into a megaphone, "It's cakewalk time; it's cakewalk time. *Evvvvvvery*body, it's cakewalk time." The crowning glory of the entire event, of course, was the Saturday morning parade, which featured a lot of John Deere tractors. Dad's best friend, Bob Flynn, owned a fancy John Deere dealership on Lansing Road, about a mile and a half from our house, which was one of the reasons Dad was a huge fan of the green-and-yellow machines. He owned both a 1040 tractor and a huge riding lawnmower and bought me the John Deere 10-speed bike when I was a teenager going to driver's training. There were also huge groups of kids on their own little bikes with crepe paper threaded through the spokes and Shriners in tall hats and silly little cars. Most importantly, the Morrice Lions Homecoming Queen rode in a convertible. From the time I could pronounce "tiara" I wanted to win the title, and Lions Homecoming Queen became everything I aspired to be.

Actually, that's disingenuous. I wouldn't have cared what the hell the title was. In spite of, or maybe because of, my childhood struggles with my appearance, I was determined to be the queen of some damned thing in my lifetime, and I set out at an early age to fulfill my dream. I lay on my stomach on our sculptured and uncomfortable Bigelow carpet, chin cupped in hands, gaping at Lesley Ann Warren with her huge doe eyes in Rodger's and Hammerstein's *Cinderella*, and swooned. I wanted the fluffy dress and the admiration, the crown and the respect.

Maybe every state bestows dubious queenly honors on its teenage girls, but it has always felt to me like in the Michigan mitten, we go out of our way to burden our royalty with ungainly, often embarrassing, titles: Potato Queen, Trout Queen, Stump Fence Queen.

As a journalist working at various newspapers in my twenties, I had the opportunity—and I mean that—to cover the Red Flannel Queen, Salad Bowl Queen, and Miss Coast Guard Festival competitions.

The Red Flannel Queen contest was held in Cedar Springs, site of my first journalism job at a dismal weekly newspaper called the *Northland News*. The lampposts on the streets of the little town were, and may still be, decorated with plywood long johns, and you could buy red flannel underwear at several of the downtown stores.

When Jim and I got married, I was going into my junior year at MSU and Jim had one year left of vet school. We were broke, so after I graduated, I moved ninety miles away to work at the little newspaper and live in subsidized housing with our cross-eyed Siamese kitten, JP. Jim had given me JP as a Christmas gift the first year we were married, traveling twenty miles on icy roads in his crappy orange-and-white Chevy Chevette to adopt the little cat from a bleary-eyed woman at what was apparently a hash house.

"I had to bring him home, babe," Jim told me. "He was beginning to inhale."

o o o

While I was in Cedar Springs, Jim slept on the couches of friends or in the vet school locker room when it didn't make sense to hop in the Chevette to grab a few hours with me before heading back to East Lansing.

My first day at the paper (housed for most of the time I worked there in the same sprawling wooden structure as a free health clinic and the senior meals program) was in August 1982. By March 1983, our editorial staff of three had gone several weeks without pay before the group of townspeople who owned it filed for bankruptcy.

Living as I did paycheck to paycheck, I asked a local sewing shop owner if I could write her a ten-dollar check and have her hold it so I could afford gas for my car.

It was a demoralizing experience, at best.

But I relished the nights that fall, when I covered all the preliminaries for the Red Flannel Festival Queen Pageant, watching as high school students took lessons in poise in preparation for their big night. I was only four years older than most of those girls and admit I was completely jealous.

Just a couple years later, I found myself working for a small daily newspaper, the *Holland Sentinel*, and assigned to cover the Miss Salad Bowl Queen competition in nearby Hudsonville. The photographer assigned to cover it with me arrived late, during intermission, having decided photographing a pageant was less interesting than happy hour. Lurching down the aisle to the front of the auditorium where I sat, he faced the (blessedly) almost empty room and slurred, happily, "Well, ishn't thish a marvelous event."

Actually, I thought it was, my pageant/queen mania was so ingrained.

Flip through a family photo album and you'll find third-grade me at Halloween dressed in an old white prom dress, circa 1955, with a multitude of tulle layers and silver and pink sequins. The dress was handed down in a load of playclothes to my neighbors, Clara and Kathy. I was the only one it fit—being a junior size 9 and too large for my skinny friends—but I thought it was the prettiest of all of the gowns in the box they received from some older cousins. I was happy for once that I was so much bigger than everyone else. Mom made me a magic wand with some cardboard, a dowel, and glitter and topped the costume with a silver mask and tiara. I was in heaven.

As the day of the contest loomed I upped my daily Hula-Hooping sessions with determination, rushing out to the garage with my hoop immediately after every meal.

Time has dimmed my memory of the actual contest if not the feeling of the butterflies I had. Someone either yelled, "Start!" or blew a whistle, and contestants started twirling hoops. Was it by age groups? Were children in the same contest as adults? *Were* there adults? I have no idea. All I know is my father was absolutely correct. There was no crown. But there *were* ribbons, and I walked away with one of those, and it was red.

"You worked *very* hard, and I hope you understand you *deserve* your ribbon," my mother whispered to me, as she took my hand and we walked back to our car.

Mom wasn't given to offering praise for small achievements, so I *knew* I had made her very proud. I thought about all my hours of practicing, and I began to understand true skill, talent, and hard work, not just a pretty face and a winning smile, might be valuable skills in life as well.

Not that I didn't keep trying for a crown.

There are also pictures of me in the family album and my yearbooks on the high school football field as a sophomore in 1975 in a polyester gown my parents bought me at J. C. Penney, hair curled in some semblance of a 1940s era pageboy. I'd worn the gown in a fashion show put on by Weight Watchers at a big shopping mall in Lansing. My friend Becky and I had joined the weight loss program with her parents, and I'd had quick success dropping pounds and winning a nod as class representative during our school's Homecoming game. I'd floated back to class after the meeting held to elect the representatives and couldn't wait to get home and tell my parents. But the day after my election, a friend approached me in the hall to tell me some of my votes were gleaned because people thought it would be funny to elect me.

"A bunch of us stood up for you, though, and told them you'd lost a lot of weight and you're pretty now," she said, solidifying my already dangerous *thin is good, thin is beautiful* values. I desperately wanted to step down, but I'd already told my parents, and they had been so proud I couldn't bear to see their hurt faces. I prayed nobody would let them in on the joke and carried on with apparent joy. You'd have to look closely in those photos to notice my weak smile and my shoulders hunched up around my ears.

"You looked like a million dollars out there, Buddy," my dad told me, which made me sad but also made the entire charade feel worthwhile. It wasn't until I was an adult that I realized he probably knew. And I bet he never told my mother.

The next summer I set out to earn the Lions Club tiara. I honestly thought it was the one title I had a shot at because it depended on nothing more than hard work.

The Lions Homecoming Queen was always crowned just before the big Saturday parade, which was the centerpiece of the three-day festival. The crowning occurred in the center of Main Street, or in front of the bank, or on the corner by Don Flood's Texaco gas station. The queen candidates in the 1960s wore sateen shifts, white gloves, and either tall bouffant or groovy *That Girl* flipped hairdos, undoubtedly sprayed with the majority of a can of Aqua Net in a useless attempt to fend off the July humidity.

The beauty part of being in the running for Lions Homecoming Queen wasn't actually *about* beauty. It wasn't about talent or good deeds, either. The queen was chosen solely on her ability to shill for moolah. Simply announce your candidacy and a Lioness (a Lions Club member's wife) would drop off two paperboard canisters, each with a plastic top and a coin slot, at your front door. It was a "penny a vote" deal with two-thirds of the winnings going to Leader Dog for the Blind and one third going back to the contestant. Helping the blind or earning money might have been incentive for most of the girls who entered, but obviously for me it was all about the crown.

You had to be fifteen to compete, but I had begun planning my strategy at thirteen, and it was "hit every damn house." Each afternoon for what felt like the entire summer leading up to Homecoming—but which was likely about two weeks—I begged and cajoled Mom to drive me up and down dusty country roads with my canisters. It was 1975 and the country was still in a deep economic stagnation after the oil crisis of 1973 and the political shock following Watergate and Richard Nixon's resignation. There were probably easier times for a flat-chested girl with no makeup, a pixie haircut, and freckles across her nose chattering on about "helping the blind" to try to persuade people to hand over some of their hard-earned cash.

But ask I did . . . at house, after house, after house. Being extremely nearsighted made my pitch even more awkward. I'd been diagnosed as myopic in sixth grade, but by the time I reached high school, I refused to wear the ugly frames, which were the only ones allowed by my father's Oldsmobile vision coverage. I squinted constantly, wrinkling my nose like I'd smelled something foul, and likely stood uncomfortably close to my prey as I made my appeal.

One day, just south of town, Mom pulled our 88—a white one this time—up the dirt driveway of a new, modular home, which looked like it had been plopped from outer space onto the lot. There were no trees and no grass. The dusty yard was littered with plastic kid toys baking in the hot sun and possibly giving off sulfur dioxide. A young mother sat on the front step watching a sweaty toddler play in the heat. An infant latched to her chest, the woman looked up wearily as we slowly approached.

"Mom, I don't think this is a good idea," I whispered.

"You are absolutely correct," she muttered out of the side of her mouth. "But I don't know what we can do about it now."

I nervously approached the woman and gave her an abbreviated version of my spiel, offering a wan smile.

"Well, if you have eyes in your head, you can see I don't *have* any money," she said. "My husband can't find work, and I have these kids. Maybe *you* should be offering *me* some of that dough from *your* can, Queenie."

"My name's Patti, actually," I said, squinting and bowing my way backward toward the safety of Mom and the air-conditioned 88.

Thinking early evening might work better and people might not be so cranky, we headed north of town one night, hitting farmhouse after farmhouse, my can slowly filling with quarters and fifty-cent pieces and more rarely, a dollar. The kindness of most people was uplifting but as we approached one tidy place, I told my mother it was time to go home.

"We'll just hit this last one," she said.

I knew inside the house lived not one but *two* boys I had crushes on; brothers Scott and Boyd. It's probably worth noting, until I was sixteen and met the boy I would eventually marry, my crushes were completely and ridiculously inappropriate. In later years, looking at old photos, I would realize Scott, a sensitive artist type, was physically not appealing to me, but at fifteen, I was completely enthralled. He had a girlfriend, though, so my affections had somewhat shifted to his younger brother Boyd.

Bantam legged with long, ash-blond hair and freckles like me, he played drums for our high school band, the Marching Orioles. I'd furtively watched him watch me laughing with my girlfriends on a bus trip home from band day at the University of Michigan the fall before. Later, I'd heard he'd been asking people about me. It wasn't so much I was interested in *him* but that I was interested in anyone who was interested in *me*. Also, he was Scott the Unattainable's brother.

"Well, what have we *here*?" their father said, bemused. He stood on his front step, looking me up and down. Squinting, I could see both Scott and Boyd in the kitchen behind him.

I stammered out my spiel, my blush starting somewhere around my ankles and spreading to my cheeks.

"It's to help the blind," I sputtered.

"Dad, just give her some money, okay?" Boyd said, coming to the door, looking embarrassed.

A few months later, a friend told me Boyd was planning to ask me to be his girlfriend. I lay awake in bed praying he would. Mom was at a Women's Club meeting and Dad was watching TV. I wondered if I should go out into the living room and ask him if it was okay if I had a cute enough, ash-blond, crooked-legged, freckled-faced boyfriend. I knew I would have better luck with my father than my mother, but I still couldn't work up the courage. It was just as well, because within a few weeks, my crush had been suspended for pulling a knife on an elementary school kid on the bus. My father was on the board of education. It would never have worked. I heard later he died young in prison, but I don't know why. I don't know if he died or why he was in prison or if it was even true. All I knew was he had a beautiful, crinkly smile, and he never did ask me to be his girlfriend.

Despite all those miles logged in the Olds, despite putting my own babysitting money in my can and accepting ten or twenty dollars from my parents, I did not win the Morrice Lions Homecoming Queen contest. I came in third, raising about $210 and bringing home $70 for my college fund. I was disappointed, but I did get to ride in a convertible during the parade and sit on the Ferris wheel afterward in my long, pink, ruffled dress for a ride with the queen and the rest of her court.

Thinking the headache and nausea I experienced getting off the ride was from too much sun and my constant dieting state of hunger, I asked Mom to take me home. I fell into bed where I stayed for a week with the most debilitating case of the flu I'd ever experience. Rousing myself days later, I read a note from my mother's good friend, Connie Flynn—wife of the John Deere dealership owner—complimenting me on my fundraising and how lovely she thought I'd looked the day of the crowning.

"Personally," she wrote. "I thought *you* should have been the queen."

Me, too, I thought. *Me, too.*

By my senior year, I'd either stopped giving off an "unworthy" vibe or my classmates had matured or maybe both things had happened. For whatever reason, I was elected to the student council and named editor of our school newspaper, the *Trumpeteer*. Along with Becky and Nancy, one of a set of adorable, cheerleader twins, I was selected as one of three girls on the Homecoming Queen Court. This time, I had no fear it was done as a joke. In my role as senior class student council representative, I drove to a jewelry store in Owosso with a co-council member to pick out the tiara for the new queen.

"Just think!" she said. "This might be yours on Friday night!"

It wasn't.

Standing, freezing on the frozen football field in a borrowed crocheted shawl and the dress I'd worn to my junior prom, I heard our beloved history teacher/half-time announcer, Mr. Farenbach, declare Nancy the winner. High School Homecoming Queen was a title that eluded me just like Lions Club Homecoming Queen had.

As I aged, I realized what a futile, nebulous, and unimportant dream I'd been chasing—or at least I thought I had until Molly, at seven, received a glossy invitation. Molly was a much-beloved, outgoing, and precocious only child. In our constant attempt to rein in her sometimes overly exuberant tendencies and teach her responsibility, we'd given her a list of daily chores, and one was to bring in the mail. She was always excited to get an envelope addressed to herself, and in this case, it was from the Miss Sugary Sweet Sweetheart Sweetie Pie Pageant or a name equally stupid. We later discovered contestants received points for providing names and addresses of their friends and classmates. Someone had *nominated* her, and she wanted to take part.

"This is wrong. Right?" I asked Jim.

"I honestly don't know," he said.

"Although the brochure does say they don't allow makeup or even nail polish, and she can show a talent. Maybe this is a way to channel her gregarious personality?"

"Maybe."

"Still . . . we keep telling her it's what is inside that counts, and here we are dolling her up in a frilly dress and having her step out on a stage. Could this be damaging?"

"I think it's certainly a possibility."

"But it says here she can give a little speech."

Obviously, we took her. We bought her a white suit for the interview portion and paid for a pair of blue polyester shorts and a T-shirt with the pageant logo for the opening dance. We booked an expensive hotel room in Detroit for three nights and did everything to ensure her success, except know the first thing about how to be pageant parents.

"This your first time here?" a father asked, sidling up to us during an opening night meeting. "A bunch of us trade gowns back and forth because they're so expensive, if you want to get in on it."

Gowns? We'd repurposed the flower girl dress she'd worn a couple months before for her uncle's wedding.

Throughout the weekend, we watched in mounting horror as young girls—many with hair extensions and tinted eyelashes, which were apparently *not* considered makeup—pass gifts of candy and stuffed animals to the other contestants in a bid to win Miss Congeniality.

Molly made one friend, another first-timer, during the weekend festivities in which there were many rehearsals and a trip to nearby Greenfield Village and Henry Ford Museum. She and Amy wore their Miss Sugary Sweet sashes and walked hand in hand and spent the time giggling like the second graders they were. Amy didn't get any more awards than Molly the night of the event, in which the winner Irish danced and announced her name was "Mery with an 'e' not with an a" as she waggled her forefinger at the audience and winked.

"My mom said we made some bad mistakes, and next year we should get fancier dresses and I should do a dance that isn't so childish," Amy told Molly.

And she did. She kept going back year after year until, by the time she was fourteen and her mother had spent thousands of dollars, she won.

Riding up to our room in the elevator, the stress, disappointment, and long day finally got to Molly, and she burst into tears. As Jim comforted her with a hug and assurances she was *his* princess, I glared at a pageant judge who'd gotten in the elevator with us, dreaming I was alone with her so I could berate her about a contest that promised it was about good, wholesome, self-esteem building when it was the opposite.

But I took in her bloated, heavily made-up face, her swollen ankles in their sagging pantyhose drooping over her worn pleather pumps, the buttons straining on her too—snug—fuchsia suit, and the way she wearily averted her gaze from a little girl's tears.

I understood something: she'd never been a queen, either.

Chapter 12

MORRICE: A NICE PLACE TO . . .

Morrice in the 1960s was typical of many very small, very rural Michigan burgs.

The tiny community was located off I-69 (the highway that had bisected my parents' farm in the 1950s when Dad refused to sell out) between the Oldsmobile plant in Lansing where Dad worked and the Ford plant in Flint where my class took a field trip in sixth grade. Most residents either worked at one of those automobile companies, raised dairy or beef cattle, or did some combination of it all.

A sprawling, new high school was built during my sophomore year in 1975 to replace the former crumbling three-story brick building, which had been used and abused by generations of teenagers. The new school was built on land directly opposite a cornfield. Dad and the other members of the school board gave hundreds of hours of their lives to planning the new facility. They toured other class D schools with new construction and even went to a convention in Atlantic City. At fifty-five, it was Dad's first trip on a plane, and he brought me a souvenir case for my glasses on the boardwalk. All their hard work paid off. The streamlined, modern Morrice junior/high school building is still standing and still beautiful all these years later.

The downtown, though those of us who lived in the country called it "uptown" of Morrice, consisted of one long patchwork block of timeworn buildings. There was always one bar, one restaurant, a bank, a hardware, a handful of other small businesses, and a few vacant storefronts.

It's almost the same landscape as today, except in 2021 the bank left town.

When I was growing up, there was a St. Vincent de Paul store and a shuttered library. Knowing all those books sat growing dusty, Mom spoke with someone she knew and one day came home with the trunk of the 88 packed with more than thirty Bobbsey Twins books. We had to give them back eventually, but I spent an entire summer reading about the two sets of twins—Nan and Bert, and Fat Freddie and Fat Flossie—and their adventures at Mystery Mansion or Sugar Maple Hill. It inspired my love of reading even if the series did body shame poor little fictional children.

Morrice was, and still is, anchored on one end by St. Mary's Catholic Church and on the other by Morrice Methodist. There is not even one traffic light on the main drag, which, when I visit, is still beautiful to me.

Don Flood used to have a Texaco gas station on Main Street, where the Lions Homecoming Queen was often crowned, with its dinging bell when you drove over a hose. It fascinated me, attached as it was to his home. Don was a favorite of mine, always bringing me a Hershey's chocolate bar when I went along with Mom to fill up the tank.

"He does it to annoy *me*," Mom would huff. "He waits until the absolute hottest July day and then sneaks you a *melting* candy bar through the car window."

Today, Don and his business are gone, and the only

gas station/convenience store is Mugg & Bopps, located one block from Main Street.

As a community, we were almost completely homogenous. There were only a handful of minority kids in our entire school, which housed seventh through twelfth grade.

Until late 2019, just weeks before I made my trip to the Shiawassee County courthouse, I remember few times when Morrice made the Michigan news. But then a local resident lured a young man to his farmhouse after they met on the dating app Grindr. I never read the accounts of the ensuing nationwide stories because the sensational headlines included words like "gruesome" and "cannibalism" and "torture" and Molly said she'd read one and cried all night.

"Don't read it, Mom," she said. "I wish I hadn't."

Initially I found it hard to reconcile the haunting tale with the Morrice I remembered, where on summer evenings we would sit on our back porch facing the apple orchard and listen to the grasshoppers and dulcet tones of Ernie Harwell, announcer for the Detroit Tigers, as he called the games, "A swinnnng and a miss!" The Morrice where we served up sweating pitchers of lemonade and iced tea and Mom served platters of hamburgers and huge crockery bowls of potato salad to the men who came to help Dad with the haying.

Yet, if I allow myself to dig deeper, darker memories can slip in.

A friend wrote me a letter when I was away at our cottage one summer during high school, describing how the alcoholic father of a local brood of kids we knew chased them down their road with a shotgun.

When I was editor of the school newspaper, Payton—a sweet, shy guy and, like me, a creative type in a school filled with many athletes—worked as one of my reporters. He was virtually the only one of the writers who cared about his assignments and didn't ask to do articles about nail polish or muscle cars. It was 1977, and while my friends and I slouched around in Budweiser T-shirts, our frayed, wide-legged jeans dragging along the ground and causing a "tripping hazard" according to Mom, Payton wore a black leather jacket and a spiked dog collar. Innocent as I was, I had no idea it could mean anything other than unusual fashion sense until my freshman year in college when a childhood friend sent me an article cut from the pages of *CM Life*, the Central Michigan University newspaper.

The story described the life of a young man named Payton from a small town in mid-Michigan. He'd lectured to a group of students in a human sexuality class at the college and described what it had been like to be a high school student by day and a teenage prostitute by night. I was told he died a gruesome death many years later.

During a phone call home to my parents while I was a college student, they told me some of my high school classmates had been arrested for the robbery and murder of an elderly woman in an old house just outside of town.

Even as a child, I understood what Mom and Dad provided for me was different from the existence of some of my schoolmates, and I wondered if it was superior to the life I would have had with my phantom first family. Though I imagined my biological parents to be a beautiful college student embroiled in a forbidden relationship with her Chaucer professor, I knew it was unlikely. I was a ward of the court, and Mom told me I'd been in at least one other foster care home—the one that let my hair get into such a state—before I came to live with her and Dad.

Throughout elementary school, Sundays were my least favorite day of the week. By the time the *Wonderful World of Disney* theme music came on the television in the evening, my butterflies were fluttering, my anxiety was high, and I was filled with dread. I loved school and my teachers, but I had few friends outside my Cork Road neighbors, and even they usually ignored me on the playground.

My entire elementary school career was uncomfortable, but in sixth grade I hit my low point. I was taller than everyone else, and my feet were already a women's size 8. Happily showing off a pair of chunky-heeled platform shoes I'd begged my mother to buy, my neighbor Clara hesitated a bit, then carefully said, "I think they're cute, but I'm afraid everyone will say 'They're big like the rest of her.' Like they did when you got those stovepipe pants."

I adored those pants. In those lovely cream pants with the huge brown flowers, I'd felt pretty and special and *normal*. I never wore them again.

My period started February 6 of that year, when I was eleven, the day before my parents twenty-fifth wedding anniversary party. I'd woken in the middle of the night to severe cramping and a bloodstain on my pajama bottoms. Standing in the bathroom under bright fluorescent light, my mother struggled against my sobbing and moaning to show me how to use the ungainly sanitary napkin belt. To add to my humiliation, my aunt Alice—Mom's best friend and one-time maid of honor who was in town for the celebration—heard my wails and came to help. My period set me even further apart from my peers, most of whom were still at least a couple of years away from the milestone.

Then came what is forever etched on my psyche as "the incident."

I'd been allowed to leave the classroom one day to deliver the first edition of our elementary school newspaper—designed by myself and written by me and a few classmates—to the office to be mimeographed. It was a proud moment because it was obvious to everyone I was certainly no favorite of our sixth-grade teacher Mr. Dumme.

In his early to mid-twenties, large, sweaty, and pale with wavy red hair, he was a favorite of some of my classmates for his reading of chapters of *The Hobbit* whenever we had indoor recess. I enjoyed the book, also, but not as much as I would have if I hadn't been under frequent punishment, my desk placed beside his to face my classmates.

Since I was meek and respectful to elders, I'm not sure what offense he'd manufactured against me, but he'd singled me out for his disdain and derision, and my parents believed it was because of my father's position on the school board. They sat me down one night and said they could see I was suffering; they did not believe it was fair nor my fault and tried to persuade me to transfer to the only other sixth-grade classroom, which was led by a kind educator named Zelda.

But I begged them not to make me change, afraid my situation might be even worse as a newcomer in a different class. Besides, I thought my relationship with Mr. Dumme had turned a corner when he'd agreed to let me start the little newspaper.

I lay on the living room floor every night reading the *Argus Press* and begged for trips to the Bookmobile when it made its twice monthly rounds through Shiawassee County. My favorite book a couple years prior was *Harriet the Spy*, and Harriet's incessant questions and note-taking, as well as her fondness for tomato sandwiches, appealed to me. I gathered my courage and asked for permission to start the paper.

I came back to the classroom that day—buoyed by my good fortune—to laughter among the boys and averted eyes from the girls. My fringed, faux leather purse was sitting on top of my desk, not hanging on the back of my chair where I'd left it. On top of it, unwrapped, was one of my Modess sanitary napkins.

Mr. Dumme was writing on the chalkboard, where he stayed long enough for me, with burning face and constricting throat, to stuff the pad back into my purse and slouch into my seat. His back was turned, but I could see his shoulders slightly shaking.

At lunch, I eased up to another girl who was also a class pariah and sat beside her during a torturous half hour while she told me about her life as a petty shoplifter, sneaking nail polish and candy bars from a local dime store. I wasn't by myself, but I felt alone.

That night, after Mom opened my window a crack to let in the fresh country air, I stayed awake thinking about the dichotomy—though I wouldn't understand the word for years—of my home life versus my school life. It seems young for such resolve, but I vowed I would overcome the preteen traumas, which kept piling up, and I would *never* let people treat me like Mr. Dumme had again. My life wasn't much fun yet, but I dreamed one day it would be different.

In my pale-blue room facing our apple orchard, weeping cherry tree outside my window and fluffy quilt on the bed, I felt instinctively life would get better. I just wasn't sure *how*, and I was getting impatient for *when*.

About the same time I struggled with my tormentor, Mr. Dumme, the Lions Club erected a pretty wooden sign at the entrance to the village: Morrice, a Nice Place to Live.

Dad came home one night furious because it had been defaced with graffiti. "Goddamned kids!" he yelled.

"What'd they write, Mom? What'd they write?" I nagged after he'd stormed off.

She hesitated a moment and said, "They scratched out 'Live' and wrote 'Die.'"

Many years later, I realized that's probably not what they wrote at all, because by then, I knew Mom was pretty good at making up stories.

Chapter 13

A MOUSECAKE OF
BREAD AND DRIED PEAS

During a Christmas celebration in 1990, I sat on a couch in Jim's parents' living room, questioning one of his cousins.

"So, just how did you know it was time to have a baby? What's the hardest thing about it? Do you still feel like *you*? What are the worst aspects?" I asked.

Jim's poor cousin must have looked harassed, because her mother finally interceded. She placed a hand on my shoulder and said, "Patti. Lots of people have babies. Do it. You'll never be sorry."

She was right. I have never been sorry, which after all these years still comes as a surprise, considering neither Jim nor I thought we wanted children when we first got married, possibly because we were barely past childhood ourselves.

o o o

We'd met when I was just sixteen at a party held in a pole barn to celebrate my friend Clara's eighteenth birthday. I hadn't wanted to go, preferring to stay home and watch

Mary Tyler Moore and *Bob Newhart*. It was Mom who persuaded me. I'm sure she realized there would be beer and boys at the party, but she also knew I was still timid enough I wouldn't do anything too daring. She loaned me her old, quilted barn coat and told me to have a good time.

The party was crowded with students from Morrice, but a couple of the honoree's friends were from Owosso, including Jim, a tall, muscular guy with big, green eyes and long, dark eyelashes. He was dressed in bib overalls and a cream-colored Irish wool sweater and had been hired to drive the tractor for a hayride.

Jim asked Clara for my phone number and called a few days later. He was only seventeen but looked much older with his heavy, dark beard and mustache. He arrived on a snowy night in January 1976 to pick me up for a movie, missing our driveway and dumping his 1966 tan Chevy Impala into a ditch. My father got his tractor and hauled the car out, telling Jim it was no trouble. Still, I'm pretty sure I saw my folks exchange a "should we really let her go out with *this* guy?" glance.

But they grew to love my boyfriend almost as quickly as I did. And three decades later, it was Jim who leaned over my father, shaving his face for the last time, Jim's tears dripping into the lather on Dad's face.

In the early years of marriage, our careers were top priority, and we agreed we would probably never have children. We liked kids, although we didn't personally *know* many. Since I was an only child and Jim was the youngest of three, we had little experience with children and absolutely *none* with babies.

We were also very poor. Our first home was in Spartan Village. "Spartan" referred to our university's nickname, but it could have just as easily described our lodging. The two-story, low-slung, redbrick housing for married couples

sprawled over many acres of campus. Our dwelling—1629B—
was on the first floor of one of the buildings. The apartment
had only two windows, one in the living room on the front
side of our dwelling and one at the rear in our bedroom.
We had a tiny, walk-through kitchen, and the bedroom with
the window was just large enough for our double bed and
chest of drawers. The minuscule bathroom had a vent, which
allowed us to hear the neighbors screaming.

"I keep you supplied in Doritos!" was the tirade one
Friday evening that sent us scurrying into the bedroom to
muffle our laughter, faces buried in the comforter.

We used the coat closet inside the front door of our
apartment for JP's litter pan. The closet had no door, only
a curtain. (This gives you an idea of how the apartment
smelled at times.) Cats were forbidden in married housing,
and JP, obstinate Siamese that he was, often climbed under
the front blinds to sit in full view of the street, but somehow
we were never kicked out.

Jim's vet school schedule was erratic because he wove
through rotations like cardiology, internal medicine, and
surgery every two weeks. There was no way he could hold
down a job with regular hours during the school year, not
that his course load would have allowed it. He worked very
hard during the summers at Uncle Walt's flywheel plant,
banking almost every penny he earned. Meanwhile, I tried to
keep my grades up while working at the *State News* and also
at Green's, the women's store where I'd gotten a job after I
flunked all those typing tests. I'd received a Basic Education
Opportunity Grant (BEOG) given to low-income students,
and it was enough to cover all of my books and some of
my tuition. If we ever ate out, it was at Burger King on
Wednesday because it was ninety-nine-cent Whopper Night.
We each ate a hamburger and split a diet soda and left the
restaurant only about three dollars poorer. But mostly we

ate at the tiny two-seat table in our kitchen, existing at times on a big pot of chili made with canned tomatoes, beans, and chicken hot dogs. The chili was Jim's concoction; far from haute cuisine, but it filled our stomachs.

One Sunday night as Jim slept, I sat at the little table paying bills with the childish, illustrated Holly Hobbie checks I was still using up from before I was married. We had just over seven dollars to get us through until payday on Friday. Then we would have forty-five dollars from my job at the student newspaper and maybe about the same amount from my work at the store, leaving ninety dollars to last us for two weeks. I put my head down and sobbed.

Still, poor as we were, it was a charmed time. We were young, in love, our lives and careers were in front of us, and we weren't afraid of hard work. The next decade was spent working very, very hard. After graduation I progressed from jobs at small weekly newspapers to larger dailies and eventually accepted a position as a communications coordinator at a large hospital in Grand Rapids before opening my own little home-based writing and design business WordStudio. Jim put in his time at three different veterinary hospitals before he realized he'd never be happy working for someone else and decided to open his own practice.

By the time we were thirty, we were living in our newly renovated home in Spring Lake; we'd purchased an inexpensive house built on spec and slowly added a garage and a yard, then removed the pullman-style kitchen and tiny living room and built one huge, contemporary, open concept space. I had a fancy, white sports car with the pop-up headlights popular at the time, and Jim drove a vintage Mercedes sedan. We ate dinner at nice restaurants, spent time with good friends, and finally had furniture we'd purchased ourselves, not received from relatives second- and thirdhand. Everything seemed complete.

Still, sitting one evening in our gleaming new kitchen, dinner in the oven, a full day of work behind me, I enjoyed a glass of wine and watched the snow fall through our huge windows into the woods behind our house. Jim was late yet again, not uncommon as his practice was still growing and he handled after-hours emergency calls. It gave me time to think about everything we'd achieved and how far we had come. A feeling washed over me.

Someone is missing. Not some*thing* but some*one*, which led to a long conversation which didn't settle a thing, but *did* lead to me grilling Jim's poor relatives at the Christmas party, which again led to absolutely nothing for another year. We've never been accused of making decisions quickly.

Finally, in January 1992, we decided to stop using birth control. When I got my period in February, March, and April, the disappointment I felt was not only intense, it was informative. *I really, really want this,* I thought. It was a revelation.

On Good Friday, a little boy came to our door selling chocolate bars for some cause. I went to the store and bought a bottle of vodka and got out my pretty, black nightgown. We had the "world's best" chocolate, martinis, and romance, which was apparently an excellent formula for making a beautiful baby.

Molly knows the (basic) details of the story and every year on Good Friday, I call or text her to say, "Happy Conception Day! That was a very *good* Friday!"

"Ewww. Mother!" she always responds.

My pregnancy was easy and sweet and happy. I was never really ill, though I often had what I called a "fur ball" in my throat in the early mornings.

"Now I know how the cat feels," I told Jim.

"Nah, it's just gastroesophageal reflux," he said, pragmatic as ever.

I wore floral midi dresses with stupid lace collars, which made *me* look like the infant, returned to the stirrup pants of my childhood, which were once again popular, and paired them with oversized, long, wool sweaters. I bought a black, velvet cloche hat with a purple flower on the side, hearkening back to Millie's orange felt number with the pheasant feather. I sailed through forty weeks, gaining just twenty-eight pounds, feeling beautiful and like the only woman who had ever been pregnant.

Jim and I read aloud to our baby in utero often, one of our favorites being the poem "The Old Gumbie Cat" from T. S. Elliot's *Book of Practical Cats.*

The poem describes the life of Jennyanydots, who makes the mice of her acquaintance "a mouse cake of bread and dried peas."

Mousecake became our nickname for our baby, and later we would name both our boat and our LLC Mousecake, also.

"I thought you guys owned a bakery," an accountant said to us once, bewildered when we told him the businesses we owned were actually a veterinary clinic and a writing and design studio.

Two months after Molly was born, I thought I was pregnant again.

"My *God*," I shrieked at Jim. "You can't come near me again, *ever*. We didn't even think we were ever going to have *one* baby, and now there will be *two*! I can't do it! There's no way!"

Those first two months had been rugged. Molly had colic and rarely slept more than two or three hours at a time since we had come home from the hospital. My reaction was undoubtedly fueled by hormones and exhaustion, but Jim was still taken aback.

"It's soon, but it will be okay," he said.

"No," I said. "I don't think I want another one."

We never really discussed it again.

Jim would have been a wonderful father to a large brood, but being an only child, I was familiar with the setup, and I really *liked* having just one kid. Molly and I went on picnics at the park and swam in the rain. We spent hours playing with her dolls and pretending to go shopping with a basket, gathering up items from around the house and letting her "charge" me whatever she thought the going rate would be.

"One million dollars!" she would chirp happily as I asked the price of one of her stuffed animals.

And there was another big issue I saw as an impediment to having more children: my parents. When I was pregnant, we woke up one night to a ringing phone that for once wasn't an animal emergency but rather my father telling me my mother had been taken to the hospital after suffering a stroke. It was the first middle-of-the-night phone call I would get of that sort but not the last. I headed to Morrice the next morning to find Mom comfortably ensconced on the couch, sipping Vernors. Thankfully, the episode had been minor. She'd suffered no permanent damage and was enjoying a bit of survivor euphoria.

"On the way to Lansing in the ambulance, the driver said, 'We're en route with a seventy-five-year-old Caucasian woman,'" she told me cheerfully, bouncing her feet up and down under her afghan. "I said, 'Do you *have* to say it out loud? You're making me sound so *old*.'"

Mom was seventy-six by the time Molly was born, and Dad had turned seventy-four just two days earlier. Gradually, over the next decade, their health deteriorated markedly. Twice when Molly was still a little girl, both of my parents were hospitalized at the *same* time, and I ran back and forth between their rooms at Sparrow Hospital in Lansing like a demented woman trying desperately to fulfill any little need I anticipated—applesauce, more towels, flowers, a *Detroit Free Press*. I'm sure it was highly annoying to them. There were heart surgeries and knee replacements, bouts of pneumonia, ulcers, gout, gallbladder removal, colon resection . . . and each time I would have to leave Molly and Jim to travel the one hundred miles to Lansing to try to help my folks.

"Did the fact you were adopted have anything to do with you only having one child?" a friend asked me recently.

"Oh, gosh no," I replied without even considering.

Maybe it did, though. Maybe the adoption wasn't a factor, but being adopted by *my* parents actually made more difference than I ever realized. Through no fault of theirs, they were so much older when they were able to bring me into their lives. Perhaps if they'd been younger, I'd still have been open to the possibility of taking on more responsibility during my own midlife years.

It's thought-provoking. But it's not something I mourn.

I had everything.

Chapter 14

FIRST FAMILY

Twice in my life I've felt prescient, both times because of Molly. When I was pregnant with her, I saw a Gap Kids commercial featuring a little girl with a halo of red curls. She wore striped leggings. I gasped when I saw the child, suddenly knowing our kid would look *just* like her. I didn't tell anyone because it made no sense at all; my hair was mahogany, and while it was thick and wavy, it certainly wasn't curly. Jim's hair was brown and wavy, as well.

While my pregnancy was seamless, my labor was intense—fifteen hours of contractions followed by four hours and forty-five minutes of pushing. Noting my fatigue as Molly finally began to crown—a C-section had been considered but an ice storm and mounting traffic injuries tied up all of the anesthesiologists—a nurse said to me, "Just a few more pushes, Patti. C'mon, you have *got* to see this curly red hair."

Four months later, Kristen visited her goddaughter for the first time, bringing an armful of gifts, including a pair of striped leggings and matching shirt from The Gap. My vision was complete.

The next time I knew something with as much certainty was when Molly was a sixteen-year-old high school junior heading to her first prom. Her date was six-foot-four, handsome, and lanky, a guy named Erik. She told us he was just a good friend. Already signed up for the National Guard after graduation, his manners were impeccable. Standing around our living room waiting for all of their friends to assemble for photos, he smiled at me and asked if he could please have a glass of water.

I thought, *Oh my God. That is the guy Molly is going to marry.*

I told a few of my friends about the incident, and they all scoffed. It seemed unlikely my liberal, health nut, vegetarian, Kate Spade/Lilly Pulitzer-loving clotheshorse would end up with a conservative and frugal farm boy who lived on potato chips, ice cream, and red meat and cut off the toes of his old sneakers to make summer "sandals." Still, it was a feeling I nursed. I really liked Erik, he was a good person, and something about him with my daughter seemed . . . inevitable.

When shortly after prom Molly endured six weeks of illness and numerous ER visits, MRIs, upper GIs, and lower GIs culminating in a ruptured appendix, Erik was one of her first visitors at the hospital. Shortly after, though, they grew apart, fought, stopped speaking, and dated others, though it might not have been in that order.

Then while she was enrolled at a Michigan State University Study Away program in New Orleans during her sophomore year in college, Jim's mother, Doris, died. Molly made a weeklong trip home for the funeral to find her parents holed up with a raging flu. She reconnected with her old high school pal, went out to catch up with him over ice cream, and before returning to NOLA, winked at me and said, "Mom, are you mad because I kissed a Republican?" They were married four years later.

I wouldn't say I felt *as* sure about unsealing my adoption file as I had about what Molly would look like or her relationship with Erik, but there was certainly *something* leading me forward. It began in the winter of 2018 when I received my Ancestry.com report.

The genetics test had been a gift from Molly for Christmas 2016. She'd always harbored more interest in my origins than I thought I did. As a child, she adored Grandma Millie and Grandpa Jim's cozy house, where a spare bedroom was always decorated with my old dolls, each holding candy or small toys in their stiff, outstretched plastic hands when she arrived for a visit. She loved games of hide-and-seek, bedtime stories, and rides on the John Deere lawnmower with Grandpa Jim. He had sold his beloved 1040 tractor when he and Mom moved from the Cork Road house to be closer to the highway in the event they needed an ambulance.

Molly would have never wanted her beloved grandparents to sense her innate curiosity about her genetic roots. Still, it was there.

Truthfully, I wasn't very interested, and after I thanked her for the gift, I packed it away both figuratively and literally. We were planning Molly and Erik's wedding at the time, and two weeks after the joyous celebration, we began loading up our belongings and furniture and memories of twenty-three years to move a mile and a half away to the waterfront home of our dreams. It was a time fraught with stress, hard work, and emotion. I forgot about the test until almost a year later when I came across it in a still-unpacked box and guilt overtook me.

I keyed my code into the website, spit into the tube, threw the sample in the mailbox, and finished the last of the unpacking. I assumed I already knew everything I would ever know about my biological parents because by this time, I *did* know a few things and had actually even *met* some of my half-siblings. They were the ones who first told me my biological mother's name was Lois and that my father was a man named Mason Ellwood. If I wanted to know more, they told me I could always contact a woman named Mable Springer, Mason's much younger half-sister who still lived in Owosso.

Mable was sweet-faced and pleasant and about fifteen years older than me. I reached out to her on social media to ask her if she could tell me more about Mason. She was polite and glad to oblige but told me her half-brother was not my father. She didn't believe he was the father of *any* of Lois's kids. Mason, known as "Whitey" for his platinum hair, was kind-hearted and sweet-natured but also a drunk. He had also been told he had too low a sperm count to father children.

"I'm very glad to be your friend," she told me kindly. "But I'm not your aunt."

I didn't believe her. Then I got my test results.

Chapter 15

I KNOW WHO YOU ARE

Inevitably, when people learn I found my biological families, their curiosity is piqued and they want to know the "how." My stock response is something like, "Well, I found my biological father's family thanks to the human genome project in 2018, but I'd *already* found my biological mother's family back in 2004. It's a story *way* too convoluted to even try to explain." It's just the easiest thing to say because I'm sure they'd think I was strange if I told them it could all be tracked back to a severe case of menstrual cramps. It had been a stressful time, even without the monthly discomfort. Our good friend Jackie's father had just died, and she was grieving and dealing with an irascible mother. Soon after her father's death, Jackie set out from the small city of Fremont — home to Gerber Products Company, manufacturer of the baby food — to drive the forty-five miles to the larger city of Grand Rapids to help make funeral arrangements. Suddenly she was overcome with nausea. Thinking it was brought on by nerves and stress, she pulled the car over to recover but became violently ill. She turned around and drove herself back home. She was admitted to Gerber Memorial

Hospital and almost immediately underwent an emergency appendectomy. She was weak, sick, and sad because she ended up missing her father's funeral.

Jim and I visited her in the hospital, taking her husband Dick — Jim's best friend and Molly's godfather — a Subway sandwich, which he ate sitting hunched in an uncomfortable fiberglass hospital waiting room chair. Something about the imagery of seeing our dear friend frightened, alone, and worried about his beloved wife just got me. I was already forty-four years old, but it was the first time life's inevitable changes and overwhelming losses smacked me in the head.

On a windy, stormy day later in the week, unable to focus on the school district newsletter I was designing at work because of the white-hot clenching of my internal organs and the mental anguish I was feeling, I noodled around on the internet and saw an ad for a magazine geared toward teenage girls. I flashed on something that had happened when I was fifteen.

Reading sprawled as always on the living room floor, I'd come across an article about a newly crowned beauty queen (no surprise I was reading *that*) who had been adopted. The queen expressed her love for her parents so eloquently, I ran to find my mother and read it to her, my voice quavering with emotion. As usual, during one of our potentially life-altering talks, she was puttering in the kitchen.

"That's how *I* feel, Mom," I said, teary eyed.

"You know, there's something I should probably tell you," she said.

My mind raced and, of course, ended up in an unrealistic place.

"Mom! Are you telling me this girl, this *queen*, is my sister?"

Her lips quivered a bit and her eyes twinkled, but she held herself together and told me no, but I did *have* sisters.

"I thought you should know because you're getting older and maybe one day you'd be curious. Maybe you'd like to meet them," she said.

I wasn't interested at all, but then my curiosity got the better of me, and I asked her to share at least a little bit of what she knew.

"You know how nice Dorothy LeValley has always been to you?"

Dorothy *was* nice. Like my mother, she was a member of the Morrice Women's Club and also of our church. Dorothy was married to Clyde, a local real estate agent and the tallest man I'd ever seen. They owned a bucolic farmhouse on the "other side" of Cork Road from where a two-lane highway bisected the countryside. I knew the couple had several children, but the youngest was several years older than me and the oldest was grown.

"Well, Dorothy's sister adopted your two sisters," Mom continued.

She told me one of the girls was two years older than me and the other was four years older. They'd grown up near Owosso, and one time when I was a toddler, they'd seen me at the Morrice Homecoming and recognized me, which she admitted had worried her.

"I just thought you should know," she said. "Maybe one day you'd like them to be in your wedding."

I thought it was highly unlikely I'd invite strangers to be a part of such an important event, but the kitchen/teen magazine/beauty queen conversation coupled with the learner's permit/old-biddies-at-the-hospital incident of about the same time was likely the first turning point in piquing my curiosity . . . except I didn't realize it at the time.

I thanked Mom for the information, assured her it meant little to me, and went back to reading about steaming your face over a bathroom sink and looking at ads for May-belline mascara and Love's Baby Soft cologne.

Two or three years later, when I started dating Jim, I hopped in his car to go to a movie one night and quickly fumbled in my purse to drag out an engagement announcement I'd surreptitiously clipped from the pile of Owosso *Argus Press* papers Mom and Dad kept in the garage to ultimately be bound with binder twine and carted to the "dump."

"Look at this!" I said.

"An engagement announcement?"

"Yes, but look at the girl! She looks *just* like me, and she's *four* years older!" I'd already explained the "I have two sisters out there someplace" story to him.

Jim didn't seem to agree on the resemblance, but I ignored his frown. I had the name of the young woman, and my parents had an Owosso and environs phone book. I carefully copied down every person in the book with her last name and carried it in my wallet for several years. But I never was brave enough to make the call and eventually threw away the paper.

It didn't matter, because once again, whether by honest mistake or in a last minute "on second thought" act of minor subterfuge, the "facts" Millie told me were wrong. It was common. Mom would make a declarative statement, be proven absolutely incorrect, and still stand by her point.

"Your cousin Kari was adopted also, you know," she told me once, when I was a young adult.

"She was?" I said. "But it's impossible. She looks *just* like her father."

"That happens sometimes," Mom said. "You know how sometimes people say you look like Dad or I."

It was true. They did, and I took her at her word about Kari until I mentioned it once at a baby shower in front of both my mom and my cousin Peggy, one of Kari's aunts.

"But Kari isn't adopted, Aunt Millie," Peg said, frowning. She's Tom and Kathy's biological child."

"Looks just like Tom," I agreed.

"Yes, she is," Mom said.

"Aunt Millie! I saw Kathy pregnant. I was *at* the hospital when Kari was born."

"Huh," Mom said. "No. I don't think so."

I'd later find out Mom was partially correct. I actually had three half-sisters and a half-brother as well on my maternal side. But the entire Dorothy LeValley's sister story was a bit off.

And that's what I began to learn that stormy March day in 2004 as I sat doubled over my computer keyboard with a steaming cup of coffee, nursing my cramps and typing into the search bar "LeValley" and "Morrice Michigan." The results were immediate and brought up the name of Paul LeValley, who was a historian who hailed from Morrice. His email address was also included. I didn't know Paul, but I did remember there were all those older LeValley kids. Without giving myself a chance to back down, I sent off a quick message, which said something like, "Hello. I was an adopted child raised in Morrice, Michigan, by Millie and Jim Eddington. They were friends with Dorothy and Clyde LeValley of Morrice, and my mother once told me Dorothy's sister and her husband adopted my two sisters. I wonder if you might be any relation, and if so, if you have any information about this? Thank you for your time."

I pressed send, likely went for another cup of coffee, wished bourbon was in it, and thought, *Well, I got it out of my system.* By the time I got back to my desk, he'd already responded.

"I know who you are," he wrote.

At the time I reached out to Paul LeValley, Jim, Molly, and I lived on the corner of an idyllic lane where the trees formed a shady canopy leading to the body of water our town was named for—Spring Lake. We'd moved to our home when Molly was eight months old and almost immediately began remodeling the two-story, modified saltbox I referred to as the Folgers Coffee house for its resemblance to a home I'd seen often in a Christmas commercial. In 2004, it was painted pale yellow, featured forest green shutters and awnings and a winding redbrick sidewalk, and had just undergone a major renovation to add on a main bedroom/bathroom suite. It was always warmly lit and welcoming, a sight I longed for at the end of a week filled with work and carting Molly to school and dance lessons. I was also always on alert at that time, keeping constant track of my aging parents and their increasing, alarming health issues.

But on this chilly Friday, I drove past our corner, knowing both my husband and daughter were already home—Jim making one of his delicious fall soups, likely vegetarian chili or cheesy potato, Molly probably in our home office chatting with her friends on Instant Messenger. It was still pouring, and I remember being cautious turning left into the driveway, four or five houses past our road, which belonged to the parents of a classmate of Molly's, Kenda and David Ladd.

I hadn't called ahead, and looking back, I'm sure Kenda had the right to look alarmed when she answered the door to find me, puffy-eyed and dripping wet under her porch overhang, thrusting out a sheet of paper where I'd scrawled the name "Ron Latz."

"Hey, do you know this guy?" I asked. "He's apparently my brother."

Paul LeValley's email included a partial family tree, with the names of my four older biological siblings: Cheryl,

Charlene, Deb, and Ron. Deb and Ron had been adopted by a couple with the last name of Latz. The wife was killed in a car accident when both children were young. Paul's aunt—the sister of my mother's friend Dorothy LeValley—later married Mr. Latz, and that was the LeValley connection Mom had made. Dorothy's sister hadn't adopted two girls, as Mom said, but she did ultimately end up as a stepmother to Deb and Ron. The family lived in the tiny town of Elsie, which was not very far from Owosso and Morrice, the town where I knew Kenda was raised.

Ever polite, Kenda looked shocked then sympathetic and told me she indeed knew people named Latz and would reach out to her family members and see what she could discover. I drove home, dried off, and asked Jim to make me my favorite drink of the time—a cosmopolitan martini. Then I sank into the couch and tried to explain to my little family what I'd discovered.

I vividly remember that long-ago night so well. We sat down after our soup and warm bread dinner to watch the movie *School of Rock* starring the actor Jack Black. My mind raced from amazement about secrets buried more than forty years coming to light and the ever-present guilty feelings about any potential hurt my discovery might cause my parents. I felt tortured.

For months, I imagined what my siblings looked like and did internet searches trying to find any information I could on them or the children Paul LeValley had listed on the family tree. Today, my searches would have been fruitful, but this was the mid-2000s and before the time of social media. I found very little but did learn Ron, the closest in age of my siblings, had three daughters. One named Olivia was only eighteen months older than Molly.

I'd soak in my big tub at night, gazing out our huge bathroom windows at the stars and the moon reflecting on the surface of our swimming pool and imagine my sisters and brother and what they were like. I feared, or maybe innately knew, their lives hadn't been cushy like mine, and it was one of the reasons I delayed almost a year before reaching out to any of them. The other reason, of course, was my parents.

While I'd been attending the liberal United Church of Christ as a kid, Jim was attending Salem Lutheran located across the street from the UCC. We'd spent our childhood Sundays yards yet worlds apart. Salem was part of the Wisconsin Synod, and when Jim was in college, the pastor first approached his parents with a warning and then unceremoniously sent Jim a letter saying he'd been kicked out for not attending communion frequently enough. It left a taste worse than church wine in Jim's mouth, and though we hadn't attended services other than during the holidays for the first eleven years of our marriage, when I was pregnant, we visited the nearest UCC to our home and joined immediately.

Our pastor was a friendly man named Don Wood, and I made an appointment to talk with him about my discoveries and my concerns. He listened to me intently.

"Honestly, Patti, you know you won't feel comfortable meeting these people without addressing this with your folks first," he said.

I'd been afraid that would be his response.

I knew he was right, though. So, when Mom and Dad came up one pretty summer Sunday, heart pounding, I asked if I could talk with them privately. We sat in our side yard on our brick patio under an arbor of pine trees with some iced tea and cookies. I gave the little speech I'd been practicing all week.

"I have a story to tell you, and it's a sad story," I said. "It has to *do* with our family, but it won't *affect* our family."

I've told the story many times in the years between getting the email from Paul LeValley and the time I decided to ask Shiawassee County Probate Court to unseal my adoption records.

"Mom and Dad listened to me so intently," I told people. "When I finished, Dad said, 'Well, I'll be darned,' and Mom said, 'I wish we would have known the circumstances. We would have taken more of the kids.'"

It was a story that beautifully displayed the generous nature of Millie and Jim and the poignancy of mere chance and luck.

I don't tell the story the same way anymore, though. At least I don't include the ending. It may or may not be accurate because, since having my records unsealed, I've learned to be wary. The documents I eventually received after my visit to the courthouse that fateful Friday in January 2020 contained more than descriptions of my dad's stutter, my mother's plumpness, and my engaging personality. They also contained a long paragraph that set my head spinning and my heart racing and led Jim to look at me with concern and say, "You know your mom and dad loved you very much, right? I knew your parents very well, and I don't believe that this is what it sounds like."

In the document, the court worker wrote my parents wanted more time to decide. After those long years of waiting and even though I'd lived with them almost twelve months, they weren't sure I was the right child for them. They weren't even sure they wanted to adopt me.

Chapter 16

AND YET ANOTHER BIRTHDAY

Hello, Patti. I had such a big smile on my face reading your email. Wish I would have gotten this a few years back. Your dad asked me to look for you before he died. He gave me a copy of the birth certificate that they give you at the hospital, with your tiny feet and your mother's thumbprint. Your mother's name is Lois Elaine DeLong; your father is Ramon Lopez. They were never married because she was married to a man with the last name Ball, who was in prison. She had four children with him: Debbie, Charlene, Cheryl, and Ronnie. She gave them up, also. I'm not sure if they were adopted or put in foster care. She gave you to Aunt Jane. Only the courts wouldn't let Aunt Jane keep you for some reason. God bless, your cousin Teressa

—Email from Teressa Rose—January 20, 2018

I'd clicked on the Ancestry.com email saying my results had arrived expecting nothing and opened up . . . everything. Under "Close Family—1st Cousin" was a photograph of a white-haired, olive-skinned woman named Santiaga

Bigelow. Next was "1st to 2nd cousin," Teressa1242, a dimpled, black-haired beauty around my age. I had no idea who these women were, but it seemed obvious they weren't related to Lois and very unlikely they were relatives of poor, pale, "Whitey" Ellwood, who I'd been told by the half-siblings I'd already met was my father.

I abandoned my laptop on the kitchen counter and wandered aimlessly around the house, staring out at the frozen lake, forgetting I needed to begin making a special dinner for Molly's birthday. My poor muddled mind sifted back through my memories.

As a kid, my dark-brown hair was uncontrollably wavy, and my skin had a distinct, warm, olive tint, yet my eyes were deeply blue. It was true my cheekbones were high, but they were almost lost in the roundness of a face treated to an abundance of brownies and Boston coolers made with the delicious Detroit manufactured Vernors ginger ale and McDonald Dairy ice cream from nearby Flint.

It was my facial structure I mostly thought about when I received the Ancestry.com email. I'd rarely thought of it since, but as I made tracks around the house, I remembered an incident from 1973 or 1974, when I was thirteen or fourteen. We were on our pontoon boat with some family friends at the cottage on Townline Lake. I was riding on the prow with Queenie, turned my head forward, and heard our friend Darlene gasp.

"Millie!" she exclaimed. "I just bet Patti is an Indian. Don't you think? Just *look* at those cheekbones!"

"No!" my mother replied, sharply. Then she shook her head and said, "No. I don't see it. I don't think so."

Had my mother known all along about my lineage?

"What the actual . . . ," I muttered, walking back to peer at the ancestry report again.

England & Northwestern Europe. . . 43 percent
Indigenous Americas–Mexico . . . . 32 percent
Spain. . . . . 8 percent
Scotland . . . . 7 percent
Norway . . . . 3 percent
Basque . . . . 2 percent
European Jewish. . . . . 1 percent
Northern Italy . . . . 1 percent
Cyprus . . . . 1 percent
Mali. . . . . 1 percent
Senegal . . . . 1 percent

It added up to 100 percent. What also added up was that Mable Springer was right—my biological father wasn't who I'd been told he was.

I quickly sent off an email to Santiaga, and when I received no response in a few days, I tried Teressa, who answered within hours. I read and reread her note, trying to absorb it all. I knew, of course, about Lois's other children and had even heard some vague stories about Lois's first husband, who I'd been told was incarcerated for a drunk driving accident which claimed the life of a child.

But I was absolutely mystified by "Your father is Ramon Lopez" and "She gave you to Aunt Jane. Only the courts would not let Aunt Jane keep you for some reason." I tried to tamp down the anxiety rising in me.

Who the hell is Aunt Jane? I wondered. *Why wouldn't the courts allow her to keep me? Where in the world did Mom and Dad come into play in all this? What have I just done?*

Teressa, who goes by Terri, and I emailed back and forth for a few days. She told me she had started her—and apparently *my*—Aunt Santiaga's Ancestry.com account, but Santiaga, who goes by Sandy, never looked at it, which accounted for her lack of response to my email. I, of course, had jumped to the most hurtful conclusion and assumed she wasn't interested in meeting me.

Terri told me my biological father Ramon, who went by Ray, was one of six children of Nazario and Leonarda Lopez. Most of his siblings had passed away, and Ray had died in 2012, but the youngest two, Santiaga (Sandy) and Eva, were still living in Owosso, where the family had moved from Texas in the late 1930s to get work in the sugar beet fields.

Prior to their move to Michigan, the Lopezes were apparently doing well and owned a home in San Antonio. Nazario was earning about four dollars a week, but there were concerns about undocumented immigrants even then. When the slaughterhouse where he worked cracked down, the family moved north.

The Michigan Sugar Company hired migrant workers and housed them in the Colony in Owosso, a comfortable enough sounding name, which loses a lot of luster when you learn it was segregated housing without indoor plumbing or heat. Nazario and Leonarda, both about thirty-three, must have hoped for a good life and a bright future when they packed up their passel of five—Isabel, Deiga (known as Mary), Ramon (Ray), San Juana (Jane), Mauro (Mike), and Santiaga (Sandy). The youngest child, Eva, wasn't yet born.

The couple apparently paid a man with a big truck to let them ride in the back with three other families and God knows how many children. They ate bologna sandwiches for sustenance on the three-day trip.

The Owosso *Argus Press* did a series of articles in 2001 about the migrant workers who traveled north to work for the sugar company, weeding fields and harvesting beets for about ten cents an hour. One of the pieces in the series, "Early Mexican American Laborers Faced Housing Discrimination When They Stayed," described the story of the

Robledo family, who first lived in the Colony but eventually aspired to buy a home in the city. Neighbors were adamantly and vehemently opposed.

According to the article, a group of women went to the Owosso City Commission on December 9, 1946, and asked the city to take action to prevent the Robledos from moving into their neighborhood. City officials apparently cited the US Constitution, and the family persevered and ultimately succeeded despite fierce objections from their white neighbors.

Another of the articles, "Out of the Colony," again detailed the story of the Robledos as well as other Mexican families who first lived in the itinerant housing camp and decided to stay in the city. Among those other families were the Bartolos, Lopezes, and Trujillos.

The Lopezes. My biological family.

The Colony was described as twenty small shacks located on Chestnut Street in the western part of the small city. The dwellings were arranged in a semicircle around what would later become home plate to Bennett Field, a municipal softball diamond. The buildings were divided into four rooms with separate entrances so each could house four families. A few outhouses were shared by the entire settlement, and the development apparently stood until sometime in the 1950s.

My cousin Terri didn't know the series of events that led Ray to eventually hook up with Lois when he was about twenty-seven, but hook up they certainly did, and I was the result. Terri was a warm and friendly woman, and after quickly asking permission from her daughter, she invited me to her granddaughter's quinceañera just a few weeks in the future. She said it would be an opportunity to meet many family members, including my two remaining aunts, Sandy and Eva.

I wasn't sure. The invitation seemed genuine and more than kind, but I didn't know if I should do it. I was fifty-eight years old. I'd dealt well enough with meeting some of Lois's other children but was sad I hadn't forged a true, long-lasting connection with them, though I think we all tried for several years. There was no common ground, too many years had passed, and we were all so different. My oldest sister, Cheryl, told me she'd spent her youth tossed back and forth between foster care and Lois, a no-win situation that left her feeling little love for our biological mother. While Ron and Deb had been adopted together by the Latz family, from everything I'd been told, they certainly didn't have the pony/cottage/ Herefords in the apple orchard upbringing I'd had. Everything I'd heard about Charlene's story was gut wrenchingly hard and sad. She died in prison not long after I met Cheryl, Deb, and Ron. She was apparently serving time on arson charges and used an alias the last several years of her life.

Still, I'd come out of it all with one huge success—a close relationship with Ron's youngest daughter, Olivia, and friendly ties with his two oldest daughters and his one grandson, as well. I thought seriously about not attending the party and just counting my damn blessings. I'd had Jim and Millie in my corner, and I convinced myself I didn't need anything or anyone else, not even simple information. I was just fine.

"I think I want to go," I told Jim.

"I think you *have* to go," he replied.

I spent the next few days reading everything the World Wide Web offered on the upcoming event, determined not to look like an idiot the first time I met my biological father's family.

○ ○ ○

The Wikipedia article "Quinceañera," updated May 2020, says, "The fiesta de quince años (also fiesta de quinceañera, quince años, quinceañera and quinces) is a celebration of a girl's fifteenth birthday. It has its cultural roots in Mexico and is widely celebrated today throughout the Americas. The girl celebrating her fifteenth birthday is a quinceañera (Spanish pronunciation: [kinsea'ɲeɾa]; feminine form of "fifteen-year-old"). In Spanish, and in Latin countries, the term quinceañera is reserved solely for the honoree; in English, primarily in the United States, the term is used to refer to the celebrations and honors surrounding the occasion."

I tried on two of my favorite cocktail dresses, one purple and one raspberry, deciding a little black dress wasn't going to make much of an impression, and made appointments for a manicure and lash extension, and commenced fretting.

Jim, however, began imagining the spread of authentic Mexican food he was about to enjoy. He'd spent quite a bit of time at veterinary seminars in Ensenada, south of Tijuana, and waxed poetic about the food at every opportunity.

"Oh my God, the tamales," he'd sigh in happy anticipation.

I've probably made the trip from Spring Lake to Owosso a thousand times in my life. It was Jim's hometown and the city where his parents lived and where his sister still resided. I've gone for holidays, weddings, showers, picnics, funerals, and class reunions but never had the two-hour trip flown so quickly and with so much nervous handwringing and heart pounding as the day of the quinceañera.

The event was held at the Capitol Lanes bowling alley, one of the city's few large gathering halls—it's since closed—and it felt like there were a couple hundred people laughing and talking inside when we made our way in from the icy parking lot. I was sweaty and self-conscious.

We watched the beautiful ceremony for Terri's granddaughter, then ate dinner (delicious lasagna and mouthwatering fried chicken, not Jim's anticipated tamales) with my two new aunts, the regal and soft-spoken Sandy and the elfin, high-spirited Eva, some of their nieces and nephews, and a few of Sandy's children. Conversation was easy because my new aunt Eva sat beside me, hugged me repeatedly, kept patting me, and squeezed me tightly.

"Ray always said 'Eva, one day you'll see Mary Ann again. You just wait . . . you'll see her.' And here you are!"

Aunt Eva brought with her a pile of timeworn and faded photos of Ray and his siblings throughout the years. There was a black-and-white picture of a slim-hipped Ray wearing a fedora, high-waisted trousers, and a "what-the hell" smirk standing beside a beautiful, wavy-haired, young woman. "Ray" and "Jane" were scratched in green ink across their torsos.

"So *that's* Jane," I whispered to Jim. There was a photo of Ray wrapped in a colorful sarape, strumming a ukulele and singing.

"*Could* he sing?" I asked the relatives.

They all laughed. He absolutely could not. After a few beers, he'd apparently also dance, pulling out his signature La Cucaracha moves to the amusement of his relatives. It was also after he'd downed a few that, throughout his more than eighty years, he would pull a photo of infant me from his wallet and tell any listener, "This is my daughter. I couldn't raise her." And then he would cry.

I remembered Dad and how he carried my high school graduation photo in his wallet along with photos of Molly playing soccer and at dance recitals. I'm not sure he pulled them out to show people, I think he just took comfort in knowing we were with him—the family he wasn't sure he would ever have for the first forty years of his life.

Also in the pile of memorabilia from Eva was an article about Ray, which had been published in the *Argus Press*, possibly as part of the series describing the lives of former migrant workers. The article featured a photo of him holding a picture of his father, Nazario, and detailed the struggle my biological grandparents endured after they moved to the town. It also discussed Ray's tough early life, an accident that maimed his hand, his work at a scrap metal company, and how even at age seventy, he rose each morning at 3:30 a.m. to clean the Rainbow Bar, located next to Owosso Taco House.

The Owosso Taco House was one of my favorite restaurants in the town. Was it possible that on the many trips Jim and I made to eat enchiladas and guacamole at Owosso Taco House when Molly was little that my biological father had been nearby? The time when Molly was five and the man came up to her in the restaurant and serenaded her with "How Much Is That Doggie in the Window," could he have been her biological grandfather? Or maybe someone he knew?

The pile of memories also included an "In Loving Memory of Ramon L. Lopez" funeral program with a photo of him in a hard hat and the dates of his birth and death: August 31, 1931– April 30, 2012. It said he was a member of the Eagles in both Owosso and Harrison, where he eventually moved, and noted, "Ray had a great love of women; he was a relentless flirt."

Aunt Sandy and Aunt Eva told me one time Ray had made a date with three women in one day and, to his chagrin, had been caught. Not surprising, then, when I discovered he'd had another child after me, a son named Paul, with a woman who was married to another man. He'd also helped raise several of a longtime girlfriend's eight daughters. All those children were mentioned in the program in a notation, which began like this: "Ray is survived by his special friend Jean Parker of Harrison, his children Mary Ann Lopez, his son Paul . . ."

Mary Ann Lopez—me. The daughter he hadn't seen since infancy was the second person mentioned among his survivors. "Do you think they named me after his sister Mary?" I asked the relatives, having gotten the rundown on all the names of Ray's siblings.

"Maybe, but we're Catholic," a cousin shrugged. "There are a *lot* of Marys."

I talked about it to my cousin, Pat, the next week. Pat is the youngest daughter of my Aunt Dorothy, who wondered why my father even went to confession. I made a *few* calls to various family members to tell them what had happened, hoping they might reassure me Mom and Dad would understand what I was doing. I tried to explain everything I'd learned and was still trying to unravel it all.

Pat listened quietly, then asked "Are you doing okay?"

"Of course," I replied. And I thought I was, but it was a lot—an *awful* lot. Most disturbingly, it had all begun to unravel additional vital stories I'd been told all my life that I'd taken for granted were true.

Sitting beside me at the quinceañera banquet table that night, Aunt Eva pulled out a photo of her holding me as an infant.

She is dressed in a pretty skirt with buttons at the hemline and an outdoor jacket, tennis shoes, and a silk babushka. She is just fifteen years old, grinning hugely at the camera as newborn me lay bundled on her lap, stiff-legged, staring up into her pretty, glowing face.

It seemed unreal; after fifty-eight years, I had a photo predating the one with permed and hennaed me and Joe, the dog, under the old maple tree.

She'd been living with her sister, Jane, and Jane's husband, Cecil, when I was born, she said, handing me an undated photo of them. Later I would learn she had been taken in by the couple after Nazario had died and her mother, Leonarda, remarried a "mean man" who didn't like children. The man apparently didn't like Leonarda so much, either, because he beat her, Eva told me. Ultimately, Leonarda also moved in with Jane and Cecil, dying at only fifty-three as young Eva lay in bed beside her.

In the photograph, Jane is slender and stunning in a cinched-waist, white, satin dress and Cecil is tall and handsome in a suit and tie. It is obviously a photo taken of a special occasion and my guess, because of the satin dress, is it may have been their wedding day. Both are smiling broadly.

"Lois brought you to our door one night and, honey . . ." Aunt Eva paused as if trying to prepare me, "your diaper was *so* dirty and there was a little bit of blood in your nose," she said, patting my hand and shaking her head. "She told Jane, 'Here. If you want her, you can have her!' Jane and Cecil, they *did* want you. We were all going to live together and be a family. Then one day, Jane dressed you in your pretty new dress and put a bow in your hair and I said, 'Where are you taking Mary?' And she said, 'We have to take Mary to see a judge, but when we come home, she will be ours forever and ever.' But then . . . we never saw you again." Tears welled in her eyes. "We never saw you again until today."

Jane suffered a nervous breakdown over the loss and later died of ovarian cancer, Aunt Eva told me.

"Honey, I think God was looking out for you," my cousin Terri tried to reassure me. "He knew you wouldn't have Jane with you for enough years, and he put you in the arms of your mother."

The story didn't jibe with the one Cheryl told me when I'd met her. She'd said Lois and her brood had been living in a garage without running water or electricity on her parents' property on an Owosso side street. She walked the three miles to nearby Corunna to work, leaving ten-year-old Cheryl in charge of the younger four children. DSS had heard, somehow, and shown up one day taking first me, then returning for the rest of the brood.

"I remember running up to the car, kicking the tires, and yelling, 'Give us back our baby.' You were only three days old," she said.

Obviously, one of the stories wasn't accurate, and I was beginning to doubt some of the aspects of Cheryl's account for a couple reasons. It seemed unlikely Lois would be back at work three days after giving birth, and also, Cheryl was only ten, a little girl, overstressed, and likely overworked.

Whatever the truth, it seemed obvious Millie's "you were the cutest little baby in the cabbage patch" story wasn't the *whole* story.

The night of the fateful quinceañera, Eva also gifted me with a photo of me and one of my Aunt Sandy's daughters, Sheila.

In the photo, both of us are about the same size, maybe eight or nine months old. We sat on a lawn, wearing puffy, ruffled dresses in front of a white picket fence.

"Sheila and I are just about the same age, then?" I asked Aunt Eva, who it turned out had an absolutely amazing ability to remember the birth and death dates of all of her relatives. She met Jim only a couple times and ever-after sent him birthday greetings on August 6.

"Yep," she said, distractedly searching through her pile of memorabilia. "You're a month older. Sheila was born November 21."

"Oh, wow! Well, actually then, we're just a few days apart. I was born November fif—"Jim placed his hand gently on my forearm and handed me a paper he'd been reading. It was my birth certificate from Owosso Memorial Hospital.

Name: Mary Ann Lopez.
Mother: Lois Lopez [obviously an untruth as at this time Lois was apparently still married to Charles Ball, the guy in prison, and she never married Ray.]

Father: Ramon Lopez.
Weight: 7 lbs, 20 inches

There was a thumbprint from Lois and tiny footprints belonging to me, and of course, a birthdate. October 19.

"But," I began. Blood pounded in my ears.

"Why don't we talk about this later," Jim whispered.

"Okay. But Jesus!" I whispered back, dropping my napkin onto my lap and sitting back in my chair. "Oh my *God, Jim.* What *year*?"

Thankfully I was still born in 1959, not before, but I felt dizzy and didn't think it was entirely because of the Jim Beam on the rocks I'd downed in two gulps to quell my nerves. Suddenly, I was back in the kitchen on Cork Road asking Mom why we'd celebrated my birthday on November 20 the first fifteen years of my life, when I'd actually been born five days earlier on November 15. Keeping my identity from the "old biddies" at the hospital might have been somewhat true, but why the further subterfuge? Did my parents *know* November 15 wasn't accurate, either? And no wonder, if as Terri and Eva told me, Ray had no luck trying to find me over the years. There would have been absolutely no way to easily connect Mary Ann Lopez born October 19, 1959, and Patricia Ann Eddington born November 15, 1959.

Chapter 17

BACK AT THE COURTHOUSE

....

Natural Parents: Patty was born Mary Ann Ball on 11-15-59. The child was made a Permanent Ward of the Court because of neglect. At the time of her birth her mother, Lois Ball, was still married to Charles Ball. Mrs. Ball gave the name of Mary Ann's father as Raymond Lopez.

—Taken directly from Report of Investigation re: Patricia Ann Eddington, (Mary Ann Ball), April 2, 1962. File no. 693—(Mrs.) Barbara Trezise, Court Worker

....

M y determination to find out what might have happened in regard to my adoption began fomenting shortly after hearing the stories from the Lopez family the night of the quinceañera. It was disturbing hearing about Jane, her heartbreak at having first thought she could raise me, and her subsequent nervous breakdown. The entire matter was tangled uncomfortably in my mind because to

question why they were not allowed to adopt me seemed
like the worst sort of treason. As I began to tell the story
and my plan to approach the court to my closest friends, I
always qualified my emotions.

"Look. I'm a journalist. I'd like to know the truth. I just
want to know what *happened* in the courtroom. Why, when
Jane wanted to keep me *so* badly and was already taking care
of me, did the judge determine otherwise? You *know* I can't
regret how it ended up. I had the most wonderful of parents.
It turned out great for *me* and I love my life *but* . . ."

I felt horrible guilt over what I have come to understand
was actually natural curiosity about my life circumstances.
I pushed through it because of the following:

1. Kristen once told me we should never feel
    guilty about something we haven't done *wrong*.
2. I'd come so far.
3. Most importantly, I was concerned about
    potential racism.

During the 1968 Detroit riots, Jim remembered hearing
a rumor there was a sign in Owosso proclaiming, "Don't let
the sun set on your Black ass." Brown people didn't seem
to be any more warmly welcomed. My new Lopez aunts
told me that when he was a young man, Ray couldn't go
into a bar without a white friend at his side. Then, there was
the existence of The Colony and the city council protests.

Was it possible a white judge had taken a look at my
pale face and determined it would be better to place me
elsewhere? Did he disapprove of Jane and Cecil because
they were a mixed-race couple? It was the early 1960s, so
I never even questioned the gender of the judge, assuming
there were a limited number of women holding such a lofty
office in our part of the country at the time.

Standing outside the courthouse, staring up at the cupola that frigid January Friday in 2020 when I considered turning around to find a cup of coffee, I had little doubt I was on a fool's errand. If I'd been asked to lay odds that I would get any information at all, I probably wouldn't have. I honestly didn't think I'd be successful unlocking an almost six-decade-old adoption record. I wasn't even sure the court would *keep* it for that long. Also, I wasn't entirely positive I *wanted* to do it. I'd spent most of my life telling anyone who asked I had never been interested in finding my biological family. It had been absolutely true, but now it had happened almost in *spite* of my efforts, and I felt compelled to learn more of the story.

When he was in his late eighties and nearing the end of his life, Dad told me he was still sometimes confused when he looked in the mirror and saw an old man.

"I feel the same on the inside as I always did. I'm not sure how *this* can be true," he said, gesturing to his face.

That's how I felt standing in the office of the Shiawassee Probate Court Registrar. I had just turned sixty but felt young, naive, and vulnerable. I was surprised I didn't need to reach up and hoist myself high enough to bring my chin over the counter.

I'd ducked into the public bathroom first and stared at myself in the mirror, imagining the conversation that might ensue, rehearsing the information I knew to be true from repeated internet searches. If neither of my biological parents had filed forms to allow the release of the records to me, I could petition to plead my case in front of a judge. I just wasn't sure what my case *was*.

"It's *my* life. Don't I have a right to know?" seemed feeble, but it was true and all I had.

I entered the probate court office, but my fears were unfounded. Three women were working at desks in the front office and listened intently to my nervous request.

"I was adopted through this court in the early 1960s and would like to see my records," I told them.

One woman who identified herself as the registrar came forward and smiled kindly. Just as I expected, she said, "If your biological parents filed the necessary paperwork, I can easily release your file to you."

"I know they wouldn't have," I told her. "My biological mother's rights were rescinded, and my biological father apparently spent his life wondering how to find me. He obviously had no idea he could have completed any paperwork."

"I understand I can file a petition to speak with a judge and want to do so," I said firmly but shakily.

She looked at me appraisingly but not unkindly and said, "Death certificates are public record. If you can bring me copies of both your biological parents' death certificates, I can unseal your file."

Two pieces of paper listing the dates Lois and Ray died could mean the end of decades of mystery. It was simple, but in that moment, I didn't know if it was possible. I knew I could locate Ray's pertinent information because Aunt Eva had given me his obituary. Knowing his birthdate and that he died in Harrison, Michigan, on April 30, 2012, I could easily obtain his death certificate.

But I didn't know what last name Lois was even *using* at the time of her death to be able to search and determine where and when she died. Still, I had spent the majority of my career as a journalist searching for information, sometimes when it seemed none was available and often when people didn't want me to have it. I was up to the task.

The registrar had given me hope . . . *scant* hope, but hope. Since she seemed like an ally, I told her about Mom and Dad and all my birthdays:

1. November 20, the day I'd celebrated until I was fifteen.
2. November 15, the date on Patricia Ann Eddington's birth certificate.
3. October 19, the day Mary Ann Lopez was actually born, according to the Owosso Memorial Hospital birth certificate.

"Wait a minute. You have *two* different birthdates on *two* different birth certificates?" she asked.

"My mother said they issued a new birth certificate when the adoption was finalized, and my name was changed." I pulled the certificate from my tattered folder. "But I guess the court also changed the date of birth, because the original Mary Ann Lopez certificate from the hospital says October 19." I showed her the date on the certificate from the hospital, the one with the impression of my tiny feet.

"I don't understand this at all," she said, shaking her head slowly. "We certainly give adoptive parents a birth certificate with the child's new name, but we aren't allowed to change the birthdate."

I spent the following days hunched over my laptop, trying to figure out enough of the Lois mystery to get a death certificate.

There were people I knew I could approach but asking any of them seemed fraught with—if not peril—strangeness. Cheryl and I had forged a somewhat friendly relationship in the fifteen years since I discovered she existed. She'd once sent me a lovely necklace with the word "sister" on a pretty charm, and I sent her flowers when I heard she had breast cancer. There was nothing *wrong* between us, it just felt superficial. Her own relationship with our biological mother had been turbulent, and when I asked her once what had caused Lois's death, she'd answered simply, "Her heart."

"Oh," I said, immediately thankful for all my vegetarian years and vowing to break up with cheese.

"Yes," Cheryl said. "She didn't have one."

I'd also met Lois's sister Roberta a handful of times. Roberta seemed like a sweet lady, but in her early eighties, she was unwell, and I wasn't overly eager to explain why I wanted to know what name Lois was using when she died. Additionally, Roberta had a wistful, rose-colored memory of her older sibling, once even telling me Lois was "a very good mother." I wasn't out to prove Lois was evil, but I also didn't think it was healthy to pretend she'd ever been nominated for parent-of-the year.

My understanding was Lois had spent the last portion of her life married to Mason Ellwood, the man I'd erroneously been told was my father. I reached out once again to Mable Springer, Mason's half-sister, and told her what I'd uncovered about my paternity.

"See, I told you," she said good-naturedly. She confirmed Lois was still married to Mason at the time of his death, was still going by the last name Ellwood by the time she died several years later at age sixty-two, and they had been living in Flint.

Lois was "no housekeeper," Mable said. And, like Cheryl who described our biological mother as "slow," Mable said she always believed Lois "didn't have all her crayons in the box." Mason, Mable's much older half-brother, had introduced his girlfriend to his family when Mable was just a little girl, and after Lois had already lost custody of her five children, including me.

Trying to impress her boyfriend's little sister and apparently prove her parenting skills to Mason's horrified mother, Lois invited Mable to spend a weekend having fun with her at her bachelorette apartment. The two decided to make matching skirts to wear to the Shiawassee County

Fair and went shopping at Jupiter, a five-and-dime store in downtown Owosso. They purchased a pattern and material in contrasting colors, but once they were outside, young Mable realized she had not remembered to get matching thread.

"I told Lois and she said, 'Well here's what you do. You go on back inside and look around a bit and when you know nobody is looking, you just put it in your pocket,'" Mable told me.

Mable was a little girl and frightened but not sure how to say no to an elder. She did what Lois told her. Days later her mother found her crying and she confessed.

"My mother told me every time I put on the skirt, she hoped I would remember what I had done wrong," she said. "And I did. I sure did."

And I will always remember the woman who gave birth to me thought it was okay to teach an impressionable child how to shoplift, I thought, once again feeling grateful about the way I had been raised. Millie might have been strict, but she was an upstanding citizen, apparently unlike my birth mother.

If Lois had kept me, what would I have become? I wondered sadly. I'd seen another photo of me as a tiny infant sitting on Cheryl's lap in a messy living room with all of our other half-siblings gathered around us. Even though it was obviously late fall or early winter, all of the older children were unkempt, wearing visibly dirty summer attire. It was a poignant, upsetting photograph because it looked like Lois was attempting to stage a happy family photo of all her children amidst disorder and gloom.

You can find almost anything on the World Wide Web, but one thing you cannot find is an actual obituary for Lois DeLong Ellwood.

Finally, through a website called "Find a Grave," I found a photo of her tombstone, which indicated she died

December 26, 1992, in Genesee County, located just to the east of Shiawassee County.

"I wonder what I was doing the day she died," I mused. But then, suddenly I knew.

I'd spent the day crying and apologizing to my family.

Heavily pregnant with Molly, I'd hosted Christmas for Mom and Dad as well as Jim's parents and siblings. My folks had spent Christmas Eve with us, and with one of our three bedrooms a pending nursery and the other spare room newly converted to be an office for my business, we'd lodged Mom and Dad in our room and spent the night on our lumpy, pullout couch downstairs. My back aching and hemorrhoids flaring, I'd struggled through Christmas Day with Braxton-Hicks contractions and with my pantyhose rolled under my huge belly every time I bent over the oven to check the turkey. When my father and Jim's brother Doug began arguing about car manufacturers—typical family gathering behavior for the two of them—I slammed the oven door shut, began sobbing, and told them what a bunch of ingrates they were. I stormed upstairs.

I remembered calling them both the next morning, December 26, to apologize profusely. Was Lois already dead by then? Did she die later in the day? Had she spent Christmas in the hospital?

She was the woman who gave birth to me, and I found it sad my questions were nothing but curiosity as I filled out the paperwork asking an online company called VitalCheck to send me the death certificates for Ramon Lopez and Lois Elaine DeLong Ball Ellwood.

I received them within the week, scanned them, and emailed them immediately to the probate court registrar.

Chapter 18

UNSEALING THE RECORD

....

Child: *Patty is a large child for her age. She has brown hair and blue eyes. Her skin is very fair and has proved to be very sensitive . . . Patty appears to be exceptionally bright for her age. She talks a great deal and very plainly . . . Patty is a very appealing child and according to her parents is well loved and enjoyed by all of their relatives and friends.*

—Taken directly from Report of Investigation re: Patricia Ann Eddington, (Mary Ann Ball), April 2, 1962. File No. 693—(Mrs. Barbara Trezise, Court Worker)

....

The envelope arrived on a Friday afternoon in February 2020 about three weeks after my trip to the courthouse. Warned by the probate court officials that my file was "small" and I didn't need to send any money for copying charges, I lowered my expectations even further about what I might discover.

But I was *still* surprised at how thin the yellow envelope was when it arrived. I set it on the counter and continued unpacking the groceries I'd picked up. Then I cleaned the refrigerator, glancing every few minutes at the envelope. I put teeth whitening strips on my teeth; we were going out to dinner, and I couldn't put off having a sparkling grin any longer, I reasoned. Then I painted my nails. I rarely paint my nails.

With Jim running late and no more chores I could convince myself I needed to accomplish, I finally approached the envelope. I took off the tape, unclasped the metal binder, and began reading. Surprisingly, there was a lot packed into the little package, most importantly in the three- or four-page Report of Investigation. The paperwork provided insight into the state of mind of my parents in the years before and *during* the adoption process I'd never had before. I read one long paragraph at the end over and over, hands trembling. I was in disbelief.

Teary, I thrust the papers at Jim the minute he walked in the door. His face while he read was at first placid, but then his eyes widened and he looked at me with concern.

"You know they loved you very much, right?"

"But Jim—"

"I know. I see it," he said. "I also don't believe it. There's an explanation. Why don't we give it a little while to settle. Let's go to dinner. We have plenty of time to think this through."

I drank too much wine that night.

On Sunday, Molly and Erik came for their weekly dinner and visit, and the contents of the envelope were passed around carefully. Everyone remained expressionless as they scanned the documents, even when they looked at the page that had affected me. They read it and I saw their eyes go just as wide as Jim's had, but then we skirted the issue.

"I was large for my age," I said, wincing, thinking of the lifetime I'd struggled with weight issues, sometimes real, sometimes imagined, but now with the understanding I'd been judged for it from the very beginning of my life.

"But appealing!" Molly said.

"And very bright," I added.

"Yet . . . 'talks a lot,'" Jim said, smirking.

"It says, 'Talks a great deal *and* plainly,'" I hissed.

Erik, wisely, said nothing.

We all noted while the body of the copy indicated I was born on November 15, the header said November 19, the fourth date thrown in the guess-what-day-Patti-was-really-born pot. Given the number of typographical errors in just the paragraph discussing my mother's family, it made me wonder if any of the document was correct.

"She has a brother William Block who lives in Trenton, near Detroit. She has two sisters, Mrs. Chester Kalegin [it's spelled Kalagian] who lives in Lincoln Park and Mrs. Jane Lyon [actually Aunt Dorothy, also known as Mrs. *James* Lyon] who lives in Garden City."

The errors were all likely oversights, so I did not let the reference to the fourth birthdate muddy the already murky waters further, calling it a one-off, careless typo. None of us questioned why the spelling of my name was "Patty," because it was the one discrepancy that made perfect sense, since I'd been the one to change it myself.

Mom always told me I'd actually chosen my name.

"I read off a list of names to you and told you to stop when you heard one you liked," she had said.

I have no idea what other names could have been on the list, but if her story was true, I likely stopped her because my cousin Pat had been known as Patty Jo when we were kids, and it may have sounded familiar to me. Not surprisingly, Mom didn't consider the appearance of "copycatism" a hindrance and named me Patricia Ann. When I asked her why she chose Ann for my middle name, she said it was because her mother's name was Anna. But I wonder now if, even as she cut, permed, and colored my hair and erased the name Mary Ann in the *My First Bible* I found tucked in the back of a drawer when I was twelve, she was trying to leave me with one small, authentic thing from my first family. I had been Mary Ann and now I would be Patricia Ann.

Reading about how all my families loved me made me smile. I was interviewed for a podcast just before I received my court documents about my adoption and search, and the host Jeff asked me if I had ever been made to feel like an outsider or an outcast as a child.

"Sure," I said. "But never by my families." This was true, except for maybe two exceptions—two great-aunts I call "the coven."

My father was the youngest of three siblings. His older brother, Frank, was the man who married Margaret (the Eleanor Roosevelt lookalike) when he was sixty. Frank never had children, but his sister Elizabeth married young. Paying homage to her staunch Catholic roots, she gave birth to seven tall, good-looking, fun-loving hellions, who went on to have sixteen offspring of their own.

Mom was the oldest of her family's living children after her siblings Mable and George passed away in their youth. Except for Uncle Bill and Aunt Dolores, who moved their passel of five to Pompano Beach when I was in kindergarten, Mom's siblings, Esther and Dorothy and their combined five offspring, never strayed too far from Detroit, taking up residence in the suburbs of Lincoln Park and Garden City.

While gatherings on my father's side were huge and took place mostly on *big* holidays like Christmas Eve, we saw Mom's family at least once a month. Birthdays, traditional holidays—even Palm Sunday—we gathered around ping-pong tables covered with linen cloths in basements, or picnic tables in backyards, or Duncan Phyfe drop leaf dining room sets.

I was the third youngest of all the cousins on either side of my family and had many second cousins older than myself. Still, I only felt like an outsider because all of my relatives were freakishly athletic. Every year during the Presidential Fitness Test, I couldn't pass the segment where they have you hang above the chin-up bar. It pained my physically fit father, who installed an old, galvanized metal pipe in the gap between two of our barns, instructed me to climb up on an old crate, then grabbed me around my chubby middle and hoisted.

"Okay, Buddy," he instructed, lifting my chin above the pipe. I probably looked like the kitten in the "Just Hang in There" posters so popular at the time. "I'll hold you until you're ready, then all you have to do is tighten your stomach muscles [as if I had any], give it your all, and stay up there until I count to three. Ready? One, two . . ." but I'd already crumpled to the grass in shame.

I thought I hated anything even mildly athletic until I was fifteen and our gym teacher assembled us into groups of four or five and had us choreograph a modern dance routine. My mind drifted back to my seven-year-old self and my tattered copy of a 1958 oversized hardcover book, *The Little Ballerina*.

In the book, young Carol, a winsome, black-haired charmer with weak legs (assumedly this was a reference to polio) and very few friends is enrolled in ballet classes by her anxious mother. Of course, she becomes the star of the spring recital, pirouetting en pointe on her renewed and strong legs to a rousing ovation from all of her new friends.

It didn't matter dancers would never be in toe shoes at Carol's young age of around seven like me. The book delighted me. I wanted desperately to be Carol, and if I could have apparated myself like a Harry Potter character into those Rand McNally pages, I would have without a look or a wave backward.

Every day I hopped off the bus, raced up the dirt driveway, hugged Queenie around her scruffy neck, dashed into the house, grabbed a cookie, then begged my mother to let me "practice ballet in my tutu." My tutu was my white church slip with a dainty pink bow at the neckline. It was only slightly fluffy, not a full crinoline, but it was the closest thing I had to actual dancewear. I had no music and even less rhythm, but I galloped around my bedroom with utter joy.

I was only vaguely aware such things as dance schools existed. Students from the Sallysue Gale School of Dance in Owosso had performed at Homecoming, and I'd watched in fascination as little girls my age in ruffled skirts and lipstick did a tap dance routine to "Sweet Georgia Brown." But I never asked if I could take lessons, and my parents never asked me if I wanted to enroll. Driving to Owosso for anything except church and Wednesday grocery shopping wasn't practical in a home where frugality was one of the basic tenets. Mom never turned on the oven to cook "just one thing," and it remained unspoken a chubby little girl without a future in dance didn't need lessons.

I didn't really mind until that modern dance segment in gym class. Afterward, I took my portable record player to the basement every afternoon, put on my Elton John, *Goodbye Yellow Brick Road* record, and heaved myself around on the cold cement. It was bliss.

I took my first ballet classes in a building located directly behind the Michigan capitol in Lansing when I was a college freshman, proudly donning my pink tights and black leotard and not minding at all that at seventeen, I was older than the other beginning students by at least four or five years.

When I transferred two years later from the community college, all of my electives were in dance, and I delighted in walking splay-footed into modern dance classes, imagining I looked like a *real* dancer in baggy sweatpants and my boyfriend's cutoff sweatshirt.

When aerobics became huge in the 1980s, I was constantly enrolled in classes held at community centers, church basements, and gyms. I started jazz and tap instruction when Molly did; she was three and I was thirty-six. For years, my class of adults danced in the same recitals, to packed auditoriums, as the kids.

Then, when I was fifty-three, I certified to become a dance fitness instructor. The Friday night audition in a strip mall studio in Brighton, Michigan, was the culmination of a year of hard work, training and pushing myself physically and emotionally to the brink of exhaustion. I'd already begun to experience back difficulties, which would result in a round of injections and physical therapy and ultimately two surgeries to fuse my lumbar spine. But despite the discomfort, I pushed stubbornly on working each week with Jennifer, the woman who owned our franchise classes, standing side by side, staring uncomfortably into a mirror, and practicing the moves and routines I'd be expected to execute during my audition.

Jen was not only a beauty and a perfect physical specimen after her many years as a gymnast and fitness instructor but also a funny, larger-than-life personality with an uncanny knack for figuring out what drove prospective instructors. She then lifted them up and away from their doubts, fears, and neuroses.

I had decided to attempt the rigorous certification process after Jen called me out in class one day and said, "Patti, when are you going to come teach for me?"

To become an instructor, I had to pass a one-hundred-question, timed physiology test, execute ten routines as perfectly as possible, and cue the moves four counts ahead. We also had to be CPR certified and were expected to make conversation about the artists, praise our students and offer safety tips.

Later I realized Jen might have just been being kind, but by then I was months into the process and steadfastly holding onto my dream. Someone had offered me a chance to *teach dance*, and dammit, I was going to do it, despite my age, and knowing I would be the only instructor with a clothing size in the double digits.

Arriving at the studio to practice with Jen after having traveled across state for a preliminary session with a quality control trainer the weekend before my audition, I burst into tears. The trainer had been underwhelmed with my abilities and told me I'd better step up my game or I was in for bitter disappointment.

"I look at you sometimes, and I think *wow*!" the woman said to me with a smile. "But then I look at you again and think . . . *wow*," she said, scowling.

It helped a bit to know she had a reputation for cruelty and once told one of our young, incredibly fit and talented instructors, "You skip like an elephant!"

"I'm just not sure I can do this," I sobbed to Jen.

"I told you about Beth's reputation, Patti," Jen said. "She can be ruthless. You're not the first person who has cried after coming back from a workshop. You knew going in she wouldn't be warm and cuddly. What's really bothering you here?"

It tumbled out.

"All my life I haven't been able to face rejection. For every adopted kid, the first thing that ever happened to them was they were *rejected*," I sobbed, parroting the words of Linda the AP reporter so many years before. "If I don't pass this audition, it will be just one more example of my not being *good* enough."

Putting all the pent-up emotion into words, I immediately thought of my two great-aunts from "the coven."

I liked my cousins and adored my many aunts and uncles on both sides, but I was a natural-born suck-up and an old soul. The people I really wanted to form relationships with in the family were the *really* old people like Sister Rosina. But in addition to the wonderful nun, my dad also had a couple other matronly aunts by marriage: Annie and Ursula. They weren't sisters, but they were almost interchangeable—white-haired, wire-rimmed glasses, Mary Poppins-like black shoes, and baggy-at-the-ankle support hose. They also both disliked children. Or maybe they just disliked me.

One of my first memories was watching my mother tumble down the cement front steps at the old farmhouse, a spill that left her with a swollen, black-and-blue sprained ankle. I sat in the back of a car while Annie sat on the passenger side in the front.

"*You* did that, you bad girl!" Annie hissed at me, swiveling around in her seat, her face contorted. "If you hadn't forgotten your sweater, she wouldn't have had to go back inside, and she wouldn't have fallen down."

I was three.

When I was seven or eight, my parents left me with her while they attended a funeral. Her antique-filled home was no place for a curious little girl. I reached up to a high shelf to stroke a ceramic turtle with a head that moved enchantingly up and down. I knocked it over and disengaged the spring in its neck, which made it bobble. The turtle fell into two easily repairable pieces, but Annie locked me in the bathroom until Mom and Dad returned. I heard her meet them at the door, telling them they should "take me back."

When I was eleven or twelve, already feeling as bad about myself as only a preteen can, Annie sat down beside me on the couch and put her hand on my thigh. "Oh my gosh," she said, laughing. "What a chunk!"

When I was sixteen, and she was well into her eighties, she was walking through a local park and a teenage hoodlum knocked her to the ground and snatched her purse.

"Patricia Ann Eddington!" Mom scolded as I tried to hide a grin when she told me the story. "What on earth are you *smiling* about?"

Aunt Ursula may have been more refined in her approach, but she was just as damaging. Ursula was the elderly widow of one of my father's uncles and lived in Chicago, a privileged second wife with a snow-white chignon, a fur stole, and a haughty air. She had a beautiful brownstone and oodles of money, and she put on a good show of approving of the adoption for a while, sending me pretty, ruffled, flannel nightgowns from Neiman Marcus and a sweet Christmas tree elf I named Elfie. Told she was coming for a visit and I would meet this glamorous human in person, I rushed excitedly out the front door to greet her when she arrived, eager to tell her about the highlight of my third-grade day, my first visit to the school library.

"For goodness sake, hush up, you chatterbox," she said. "Millie, for the love of the Lord what are you feeding this child? She's far too fat."

Maybe I just had bad luck with two cranky old ladies, but I don't think so. I think they just couldn't understand why Jim and Millie would raise a child who wasn't their own.

Chapter 19

A VERY NICE CAR

In March 2020, just a month after I received my unsealed adoption records and a week after I'd returned from an annual, much-anticipated, weeklong family vacation on North Captiva Island in Florida, the nation fell to its knees because of COVID-19. We'd left for our trip pondering the masks we saw people wearing in the airport, and within a week of our return, wished we'd spent the winter stocking up on toilet paper and hand sanitizer.

One month later, one of my favorite cousins would be dead from the disease, leaving behind a beautiful wife, three kids, three grandkids, and a grieving extended family. Over the following eighteen months, I would lose more relatives, Jim would also lose a cousin, a friend would lose her grandmother, one of my dance students would lose a son, and another would lose a husband.

During a phone call "happy hour" four days after Michigan's governor, Gretchen Whitmer, ordered all but essential businesses to close and for the rest of us to stay home, my cousin Pat said, "I wonder if this is what it was like for our parents during WWII with rationing and coupons? I wonder if they were afraid like this?"

They were. They'd spent their lifetimes telling us about it, and when they weren't telling us, they were showing us. Mom's suds saver, coupon clipping, and all her rules and overprotectiveness were an attempt to keep us safe and happy. She was trying to preserve the beautiful life she and Dad had fought so hard to achieve.

Jim and I talked often about my parents during the pandemic, sorry they were gone but happy they didn't have to endure the COVID-19 pandemic. We had friends with loved ones residing in assisted care facilities. We heard about sadness and fear for both the residents and the families who were unable to visit. My mother's decline and death had been rapid, but my father would have been one of those isolated in a care facility if he was alive.

○ ○ ○

I had been alone with my mother when she died two days after Thanksgiving in 2007. I'd sat with her for days, while Jim and Molly and all our relatives drifted sadly in and out of her hospital room. At ninety-one, her colon had ruptured as she played euchre with Dad and some new friends they had met at Independence Village in East Lansing, where they'd moved just six months before. They'd been heartbroken to leave Morrice but determined to have one more fresh start on their own terms.

After undergoing emergency surgery, she lingered in the hospital for ten days. I'd forced Molly and Jim to have Thanksgiving with his parents and siblings and held my mother's hand while she tried to force down a bit of turkey and mashed potato mush. My dinner on the day set aside to celebrate gratitude was a cup of stale coffee and a dry, crumbly, no-bake cookie from the hospital cafeteria. She died at 5:45 a.m. the following Sunday after a restless and uncomfortable night, in which I swabbed her mouth repeatedly with a little pink sponge on a stick and reminded her how much I loved her and what a good mother she was. She nodded to acknowledge she heard me, but she was obviously not at peace.

"Well, goodbye to this horrible life," she said at one point, shaking her head sadly, eyes closed.

"Oh, Mom!" I gasped, shocked. "It was pretty good, wasn't it? We had some fun, some good times, didn't we?" She nodded slightly, then fell into troubled breathing. I'd thought I was ready, prepared, and strong, but I rushed to the door and called for help.

"What's wrong?" a nurse yelled from down the hall.

"My mother is dying!" I screamed. "And I don't want to be alone."

Two weeks after Mom passed away, my father took the first of many falls. The Parkinson's disease he'd been diagnosed with a few months earlier kicked into high gear with his grief, and he and I spent the next two and a half years at war against the horrible disease. I've lost track of the number of falls—he broke his hip and foot once tripping over the leg of a card table as he valiantly attempted to resume playing euchre with his friends—and emergency room visits, though I can remember at least twelve spread between two different hospitals. I spent hours trying to find anything—ointments, tinctures, a contraption to help him put on his socks, softer socks, a medic-alert device, shirts with velcro, shoes with velcro, candy, movies, digital display photo frames filled with images of happier days to bring a few moments of relief to his painful body and psyche.

The first year after Mom died, I put forty thousand miles on my car driving between my home and Independence Village an hour and a half away. To make it up to me, Dad gave us $25,000 of his hard-earned savings to put toward the car of our choice. A career GM man, it must have pained him when I chose a huge, hulking, blue Ford Flex with a white top, a car one of my cousins called "the hearse." If it bothered him, he never let it show. "This is a nice car," he'd say, patting the interior. "A real nice car."

I kept the Flex for almost ten years and sobbed when I knew it was time to trade it in. I looked at every fancy SUV on the market—Mercedes, Jaguar, and Lexus—and ended up buying another Flex. It reminded me of my father.

In late July 2010, Dad made phone calls to friends, saying goodbye, planning his funeral, and determining where memorial contributions would be sent. We discussed his wishes and when I told him, through tears, the staff at his assisted living residence had suggested hospice care, he asked me what I thought and if it would be too hard on me.

"Dad, you've always made good decisions," I said. "This is up to you."

He nodded and said, "Let's do it."

He was in the hospital once again when he made the decision. He'd fallen on a Saturday night in the restroom. Molly, just getting ready for her senior year in high school, and I were in training to take part in a sixty-mile walk to benefit the Susan G. Komen Foundation. Since we were obligated to train for it on Sunday morning, Jim sat at Dad's side until I could make it to the hospital in the early afternoon. I stayed with him the rest of the day leaving only to get him a cookie, ice cream, and anything to try to bring him comfort even for just a few moments. Getting ready to leave, I kissed him on the forehead, held his hand, and made a judgment call.

"Dad, do you know what . . . a thong is?

He looked at me, raised an eyebrow, and nodded.

"Well, we did the training walk this morning, and the minute we came in the door afterward, Molly rushed to the bathroom. When she came out, she gave a big sigh and said, 'Never ever walk twelve miles in a thong!'"

The corners of his beautiful hazel eyes crinkled, and I listened to my father belly laugh for the last time. He entered hospice the next day and died within the week.

○ ○ ○

Ten years later when everything unfolded—when I discovered my real birthday, found an entire new family to love, and Mary Ann Lopez shyly stepped out behind the filmy veil of years of uncertainty and said, "Hello, I've been waiting to meet you," the old guilt resurfaced. If I told the story about Ray carrying a photo of me in his wallet, telling people about the daughter he couldn't raise, I was so, so careful to say, "My *biological* father."

I didn't want anyone to think I didn't love, respect, and cherish Dad and *miss* him every day of my life.

I never bothered to mention Lois because she embarrassed me.

"Who is *that* guy?" I'd asked, gesturing to the corner of a family photo Lois's sister Roberta showed me during a lunch date.

"That's Lois," Roberta said. "That's your *mother*."

I didn't think anyone I knew would ever confuse plain, manly Lois with my elegant and beautiful mother Millie. Every blocky, inelegant, unappealing thing I've always hated about my own appearance I saw in the photo of Lois. I inspected photos of young Ray and young Jane closely, praying I'd recognize some of the beauty it was so easy to discern in my biological father and his sister in myself.

It was my good friend, Teresa, who sweetly set me back on course.

"I think maybe you've idealized Ray," she said cautiously. "Because you know he was right there, at least at the beginning, as well."

A few weeks after getting my court records, I asked Teresa to go with me to Owosso to meet with Aunt Sandy (Ray's sister) on one afternoon and Aunt Roberta (Lois's sister) the next. By this time, Aunt Eva had moved to Northern Michigan. Over our salads at a little diner, we asked Aunt Sandy what she could remember about the time I was born and if she had any insight into what might have happened.

She shook her head. "No, no, I was so busy right then."

It's true. When I was born, Aunt Sandy, already a mother of three, was heavily pregnant with her fourth child, Sheila, born on November 21, just a day after the *first* birthday I'd ever celebrated. Aunt Sandy is among the earth's sweetest of women, but something in her averted gaze made me feel like maybe she did have memories she preferred to forget.

Aunt Roberta asked to have lunch at a deli in downtown Owosso the next day, bringing with her a shoebox filled with family photos.

She reiterated her belief Lois was "a good mother," then told us she and her husband had visited unannounced shortly after the court interceded and her five children had been taken away to find Lois frazzled with the oven door open and the gas turned on.

"Did you think she intended to hurt herself?" Teresa asked gently.

Roberta cast her eyes down, lowered her chin, and nodded slightly, then looked back into her shoebox and found a photograph of herself as a young woman in a pretty dress. "Oh, look here!" she said.

The visits with Sandy and Roberta only served to muck up the story more, leaving me unsure of just what the relationship with Ray and Lois was at the time of my birth.

Ray was only twenty-seven when I was born, and I was—to the best of anyone's knowledge—his first child. It was a few years later when he had the affair with a married woman, and she became pregnant with my half-brother. I'd learned from my Lopez cousins that Ray had spent the last twenty years of his life with a woman who lived in Harrison, only a tad north of the center of the state but north *enough* to make any Michigander think about flannel shirts, whitetail deer, and bonfires. The woman was the first person listed as a survivor in Ray's obituary: Barbara Jean Parker.

Chapter 20

NOBODY EXCEPT RAY

"Honey, I don't think you need to get dressed up. It's going to be hot and humid again today," I said, watching Jim pull on a crisp shirt and khakis. "Just wear a polo and some shorts. It's going to be just us. Be comfortable."

"That's okay," Jim said, sliding his closet door shut. "It's about respect."

Jim was a skilled general practice veterinarian who decided in his mid-forties to switch career trajectory and specialize in veterinary dentistry. In the early summer of 2021, he was sixty-two and still working sixty-hour weeks repairing jaw fractures and conducting complicated root canals at his thriving Spring Lake practice. He also instructed students in dentistry most Wednesdays at the Michigan State University Veterinary Teaching Hospital. He'd finally decided to gift himself a break from the tedium of the weekly two-hundred-mile round trip and take every other Wednesday off to relax. But here it was, a Wednesday, and he'd readily agreed to drive almost three hundred miles to help *me*.

My husband is the kind of man who wouldn't dream of taking a bite out of his dinner until everyone at the table is served. He opens doors for women, adores babies, children, old people, and animals. He gives magnificent gifts to those he loves and generous donations to good causes. An avid reader, he loves nothing more than an afternoon on our deck with a book, glancing up on occasion to look out over the bayou where we live to note a bald eagle overhead or a turtle rising from the water. He'll say, "What a beautiful day," and continue reading.

He is brilliant at his job and so handsome his staff has had to fend off many admirers on his behalf over the years. He never told me these stories—they did. He is a gentleman in every sense, and his family knows that while he has worked hard to have the trappings of a good, comfortable, and peaceful life, if it were all stripped away tomorrow, the only thing he would care about keeping would be us.

So I wasn't surprised he wanted to travel to the northern Lower Peninsula with me to Harrison on an errand set in motion months before with a phone call from my biological father's longtime girlfriend Barbara Jean.

We were taking the trip to bury Ray . . . nine years after he died.

I'd called Kristen ten or eleven months earlier, knowing she could probably help me as I struggled with a way to reach out to Barbara Jean and find out as much as she could tell me. I realized what she told me might complicate the information I already had even more but also speaking with her would be a fait accompli.

"So, essentially, you're going to bribe this lady to talk to you," Kristen said when I called her to plead for help. Kristen spent most of her career as a copy editor, and I needed to tighten up my rambling request.

"Hello, I'm the illegitimate daughter your lover lost

somehow shortly after I was born, and I'd really like to talk to you, even though you maybe don't want to talk to me, so here's my phone number, address, and email. Please, please, please get in touch!" A condensed version would accompany a big bunch of sunflowers.

"I guess it could be considered a bribe. I just want to get her attention. Is it wrong?"

"Would it matter?"

"No."

In the years since I'd learned Ray's identity, I'd heard quite a few tales about the man, and I'd estimate 98 percent of what I'd heard had been positive. It sounded like he was loving, if flawed, and I was curious to learn more of his story. But I kept reminding myself that while he was a biological parent, he was not my *real* father. He could never and would never replace Jim Eddington.

Ray was a man I'd only seen in photographs—a guy with dark skin, a wrinkled forehead disturbingly like mine as I age, and shiny, floppy, black hair. Aunt Eva had given me a pile of photographs, including several of him with his siblings and one picture possibly taken in the mid 1990s based on his Members Only–style jacket and Barbara Jean's oversized eyeglass frames. But the most poignant photo was of him sitting on a couch against a colorful afghan, wearing a blue work shirt embroidered with "Ray."

On the back of the photo was scribbled, "Ramon Lopez (Ray) at Barbara's house in Harrison before he passed away."

I smiled a little when I first saw it, thinking, *Thank God it wasn't after*, but I think we can assume what the scribbler meant was *just* before he died.

Kristen and I debated whether Barbara Jean, being in her later seventies, would respond to me better with a phone number, email, or street address. I decided to include both my phone and email. Essentially my message had been condensed to stating I was Ray's daughter Mary Ann, now known as Patti, hoped I could speak with her, and asked her to contact me. I went through a national floral distribution company because Harrison was a small town like Morrice, and I didn't want the message becoming the fodder of gossip. *I didn't want the old biddies at the hospital trying to figure out who you were.* I arranged for the flowers to be sent on a Tuesday in August 2020.

"I figure one of two things will happen," I told Jim. "Either she will contact me right away, or she'll ignore it. Maybe she's afraid I will *want* something. Maybe I should have told her I *don't* want anything except information?"

Barbara Jean called me within an hour of my inbox alerting me the bouquet had been delivered. I saved her message.

"Hello, Patti, this is Barbara Jean. I used to go with your dad. Thanks for the sunflowers. They are beautiful. I called to speak with you. My number is . . . maybe you can call me back when you get this message. Okay. Give me a call, and I'll gladly talk to you. All right. You have a good day."

Her voice was kind, and she seemed sweet and self-deprecating, yelling to her daughter to remind her of her phone number while she was leaving the message. "I can't even remember my own phone number. Bad, huh?" she said laughing.

We played phone tag for twenty-four hours before finally connecting.

She told me she met Ray at the Eagle's Club in Harrison on karaoke night one Saturday around Halloween in the early 1990s. After she'd stepped from the stage, he motioned her to a table he was sharing with his brother Mike, who had a cabin in the area. He complimented her voice and asked her to sing "He Stopped Loving Her Today" by George Jones.

"He said it was his favorite song," she told me.

When she had finished singing arguably the saddest torch song ever written, he asked for her number and called her the next day, initiating what sounded like a happy, twenty-year relationship.

"He loved you so much," she told me. "You were the world to him."

Barbara Jean agreed with Lois's sister, Roberta, who told me Ray was living with Lois at the time of my birth, though other relatives have disputed the scenario, saying while they lived in Owosso the couple never officially lived together. His work with a metal shop eventually sent him to St. Paul, Minnesota, and he took Lois and her brood of five along. He returned from work one day to find us gone, on a bus back home to Owosso.

Ray had called his sister, Jane, and instructed her to meet the bus and take me.

It's unclear what actually happened, but my guess is Lois initially shunned the offer and then eventually relented, showing up at some point later on Jane's doorstep, as Aunt Eva and the other Lopez relatives recalled.

If you want her, you can have her.

"Jane would write to Ray every week and tell him what you were doing. But she was lying to him," Barbara Jean said. "He surprised them after you'd been gone from Minnesota for about six months with a visit, and when he showed up, there was a party for someone. Everyone was drinking and singing and then he walked in and everyone got silent. He said, 'Where is she? I want to see the baby.' And Jane said, 'Have a seat, Ray. The baby is gone.'"

Jane told Ray court officials had taken away Lois's other four kids because of neglect. "Lois said, 'You might as well know I have another one,' and told them you were with Jane and Cecil," Barbara Jean relayed.

I spoke with her for maybe a half hour and wished her luck on some upcoming surgery. She gave me the names and contact information for a couple of her daughters and thanked me again for the gift.

"When I got flowers, I was so surprised," she said. "Nobody else has ever sent me flowers in my entire life. Nobody except Ray."

Chapter 21

TAMPERING WITH
A GRAVE IS A FELONY

"Hell no. I'm not doing it. Leave me out of it," my son-in-law, Erik, said, staring at me wide-eyed and smacking his cherry Pepsi down in disbelief on the tabletop of the Spring Lake Country Club where we were eating dinner on the patio.

"So, please understand it's not actually a really fancy cemetery according to his girlfriend," I told Erik. "Apparently it's out in the middle of nowhere. Barbara Jean said nobody will probably even be there, and I'm going to take some geraniums or whatever so if anyone *does* come by, they will probably think we're just planting flowers. It will take ten minutes, maybe less."

I was asking Erik for help burying Ray because part of his job as a public works employee meant he was familiar with the ways small municipality cemeteries operated. The hardest working man in town, Erik was also a Sheriff's Deputy Marine Patrol Officer and a firefighter and a former member of the National Guard. He'd entered the service right after high school. I maintained a friendship with Erik's mother and also with Erik, writing him while he was at boot camp.

When I asked him once why he'd joined the guard, he said, "Because I feel it's my duty." By the time he was twenty-seven, in addition to his day job and his work with the marine patrol, he'd also run for public office and became supervisor of the township where he and Molly lived, defeating an eighty-year-old career politician with a bigger budget and more name recognition. Erik won the election based on his reputation for honesty and his simple promise of clarity in local government.

I knew if he thought it was wrong, he would tell me.

"Tampering with a grave is a felony," he said. "Leave me out of it. You shouldn't do it, either."

"Okay, but I don't think you can call it a grave unless there is someone actually buried in it," I said. "And there's not . . . yet. I said the same thing, by the way. I said we should contact the cemetery officials and see how to go about this the right way. But Barbara Jean said they would just be confused because they already think the burial *has* taken place."

The scowl on Erik's face told me the discussion was over, so I began to develop plan B.

Just a couple weeks earlier, in May 2021, Jim and I had been hurtling south along I-75 toward Harrison after a short three-day vacation on Mackinac Island—it always feels like hurtling to me when Jim is driving, though he swears he never goes more than seventy-four miles per hour—when he turned to me, forehead furrowed with concern.

"How are you feeling about all of this?"

It had become a pretty standard question posed by every friend and family member I told my story to over the preceding couple of years.

"Fine," I started to reply, but then I remembered I probably hadn't actually *been* fine after all the emotional meetings with my biological relatives and opening the envelope holding my adoption records.

It's hard to overemphasize the metamorphosis I'd undergone. As a young person I espoused, and truly believed, I had no curiosity about my origins. By middle age, I'd connected with Lois's offspring and came to terms with the knowledge that my biological mother wasn't a woman who'd lovingly given me up so I could have a better life but rather someone who couldn't, or wouldn't, care for her children. And by the summer of 2021, I was sixty-one years old, working hard to unravel the mystery of the beginning of my own life.

"I keep meeting all these relatives and people who knew Ray and who knew me as a baby and *still* feel like they know me. They're very nice, and they tell me they love me and I know they mean it, but really we're all just strangers," I said to Jim. "I also keep thinking they feel like all of this is the way it *should* have been . . . me being a part of Ray's life. I don't want to hurt their feelings, but obviously I think it turned out the way it was supposed to turn out. Mom and Dad were my parents. I can't imagine any other scenario."

Barbara Jean had called me in mid-March 2021, several months after the first phone conversation. I'd sent her cards for Thanksgiving and Valentine's as well as a gift at Christmas, but I hadn't heard from her again and resigned myself I'd learn nothing more. I wasn't upset. She'd had two decades with Ray, and they sounded like pleasant, happy years. But I knew firsthand just how hard it was to form a true, meaningful relationship based on stories and hearsay. I didn't blame her if, curiosity sated, she'd decided to call it good. Then she left me a voicemail.

"Patti, this is Jean. Um, I know you as Mary Ann, but I wanted to talk to you about your dad. So if you could call me back I'd sure appreciate it. Thanks for the beautiful Valentine's card. That was a surprise for me. I liked it. It was the only one I got."

I called her back, assuming she'd thought of another Ray story I should know, but it wasn't the reason. She didn't just want to *tell* me about Ray—she wanted to *give* him to me.

"I wanted to talk to you because I've been thinking, and I want you to have your dad's ashes," she said.

They'd been in her bedroom closet since his death in 2012, and she wanted to entrust them to my care. Even more, she wanted me to remove his tombstone from the cemetery—she'd had it engraved with an etching of a crane (he'd operated one at Owosso Iron and Metal for many years) and hoped I'd move it—and him—closer to where I live. "I think all we need is a winch," she said.

"Do you think it will fit in the back of the Flex? Would it be bad for my shocks?" I asked Jim, who looked at me incredulously.

"Yes," he said slowly. "It would be absolutely *horrible* for your shocks, and also, we can't just go and get a winch and remove a headstone from a cemetery!"

It's a personality quirk of mine. I liked Barbara Jean on the phone, and I've always been easily persuaded and susceptible to try to help people I like. It has backfired numerous times, and my friends and family always seem mystified I don't ever seem to learn the lesson.

Still, I never do. After just a few minutes of conversation with Barbara Jean, I was wondering how expensive it would be to buy a cemetery plot in Spring Lake or Owosso and have Ray's headstone moved cross-state.

"How in the hell did I get in this position?" I sighed.

"Let's just go and talk with her in person," Jim said. "Let's see what is really going on here."

So after a long weekend on the beautiful island where no cars are allowed and the air is always scented with an odd, but not as unpleasant as you'd imagine, mix of horse manure and chocolate fudge, we adjusted our normal route home and stopped to see Barbara Jean. She politely told me she would actually prefer to just be called Jean. Confined to a wheelchair after a myriad of health issues, she was welcoming and proud to show off photos of her eight daughters, all born before she met Ray, and her numerous grandchildren and great-grandchildren. In all, she said, her immediate family totals more than one hundred people. She'd had her first daughter when she was only seventeen.

"She was born in 1959," Jean said with a smile. "Same as you."

While her relationship with Ray spanned two decades, he'd only actually lived in Harrison with her for the last few years of his life following his retirement. He loved the small, rural city with a population of just over two thousand. Ironically, after they'd waited so long to be together, during those last years, Jean began experiencing health issues, which necessitated Ray caring for her. "He was so kind to me. He was a good man. He bought me that TV," she said, pointing to a modestly sized flat screen on the wall of her bedroom where we sat visiting. The lung cancer which took his life spread quickly, and he was gone within six months of his diagnosis.

A small insurance policy paid for Ray's headstone and service, but Jean told us she had never been able to bring herself to have his remains buried. They were still in her bedroom.

"Let me try to figure it out," I told her, which is how I got into the ill-fated conversation with Erik.

Eventually, I decided to contact the funeral home that had handled Ray's service.

"I know it's strange he died in 2012 and hasn't been buried yet," I said apologetically.

"You know, it really isn't," the lady who answered told me. "Honey, we've seen it all."

She directed me to the Summerfield Township offices, where a friendly township clerk named Jaclyn listened politely to my story and reaffirmed the delay in burial was "no big deal." She went out to the cemetery on her own time and found Ray's grave, and we set a date and time for his internment: June 30 at 1:00 p.m. For $175 and one day out of our lives, Ray would be officially and finally at rest.

Prior to this I had, or believed I had, hard-won familiarity with all things regarding cemeteries and burial.

Most people I know seem to fall into the "visit your loved one's cemetery at least at Christmas and Memorial Day" or the "what good does it do, they're gone, never visit the cemetery after the day of the funeral" camp. Mom fell into the former group, and Jim's family is firmly entrenched in the latter. My father slid into another realm entirely after he retired in 1980 when he was sixty-one—"spend an insane number of hours at the cemetery every single week of your life" realm.

Later, we would all acknowledge Dad was mildly depressed after leaving his job at Oldsmobile. While his nights were still filled with Lions Club or Knights of Columbus meetings, he floundered during the day. Pictures of him from the time show a still very fit, handsome, tanned, and jovial man and had he been in a different profession, he'd likely have preferred to work another ten years. But at the factory the "thirty and out" mentality ran strong, and he'd begun working at Olds in 1950 when he and Mom moved to the farm. His body was still strong, but he'd already undergone a back surgery, would eventually need two knee replacements, and complained often about pain in his poor, thin, and bony size 13 feet. He'd long since given up tending his fields, and by the time he retired, he'd been renting them out to neighbors for their corn crops for years.

Without his job and without his farm, Dad began to flail emotionally. He was a hardworking man who'd always had a purpose and was reticent to wallow in self pity, so he started looking for a *new* purpose. Always so devout, he began spending even more time at St. Mary's, and he landed a position on the church's cemetery board.

Bethany Cemetery is located on Morrice Road just outside the village. My father's parents, grandparents, aunts and uncles, and his brother Frank are all buried just yards from the pretty, arched iron gate leading into the property. The focal point of Bethany is a small hill on which a statue of Jesus stands and where priests are buried, including Father Jordan, Dad's uncle.

Mom always took me to the cemetery when she visited, teaching me to walk with reverence around the plots, never to stand on top of the graves, and to kneel carefully when planting the Memorial Day geraniums or affixing the Christmas wreaths. My parents never shied away from taking me to funerals and internments as a child, and because they were older parents with older friends and relatives, I attended plenty. I never thought it was morbid; I found cemeteries kind of beautiful.

Dad eventually graduated from being a member of the cemetery board to volunteer sexton. For many years, the phone would ring while we were visiting, and he would dash uptown to meet with a family who either had not had the forethought to preplan or who had been unexpectedly struck by tragedy to help them pick out a grave site. If the circumstance fell into the latter category, he would always come home without his trademark twinkly eyes and reassuring smile. It was an unpaid position, but he dedicated the last years of his life and just as much passion to it as he had to his work at Oldsmobile or his service to the school board or the Lions Club.

Dad was just as meticulous and as much a perfectionist as he'd always been and would unfailingly go to check the work of the grave diggers before a funeral. One day, peering closely into a freshly prepared plot, he lost his footing and fell to the bottom. He wasn't injured but there was nothing to grab except dirt. Being over seventy and a survivor of those two knee replacements, he couldn't scramble up the slippery sides of the grave. It was the early days of cell phones; they were big and clunky and housed in a bag and only used in case of emergencies. He'd left his in his truck, so he did the only thing he could do. He sat in the corner of the grave and waited, hoping maybe Mom would notice he had been gone too long—she didn't—or someone would see his truck parked and vacant in the cemetery and come to check on the situation.

A few hours later, he heard a vehicle pull up the gravel drive, and once it shut off he began shouting. Soon the familiar face of a friend who'd indeed been passing by and seen Dad's truck but no sign of Dad peered over the edge of the grave.

"Hey, Jim."

"Hey."

"Whatcha doin'?"

"Just hanging around."

"Well, how is it down there?"

"You know, it's not so bad. I'm getting used to it."

Dad loved that story, but what he didn't love was the way the church was being governed through the final years of his life. He'd been friends with many of the priests who'd been appointed to St. Mary's and one, Father James Schmitt, who'd served for about eight years from the mid '80s to the early '90s, became one of his dearest friends.

But in the early 2000s a priest, I'll just call him Father Dick, had been placed at the parish, and it wasn't a good fit in the opinion of Dad and many other parishioners. Father Dick waged a campaign to build a new educational facility or church, I forget which, on a plot of land in the cornfield across from my old high school, something Dad found not only totally unnecessary but fiscally wasteful. St. Mary's was founded in 1891 and the "new church" was constructed in 1955. The lovely wood interior of St. Mary's was Dad's beloved sanctuary. He was a longtime usher and never missed a Sunday service. On Maundy Thursday, he would rise from bed in the wee hours of the morning to take his turn sitting in the nave to pray and reflect in honor of the time Jesus sat in Gethsemane. It seemed like a beautiful gesture to me.

But there weren't many Sundays in the last decade or so of Dad's life when he wouldn't come home from church flushed and angry, recounting the latest sins of Father Dick. His response to those misdeeds must have certainly earned Dad penance quite a few times.

"Goddamn it, Millie!" Dad would shout, pounding his fist on the table, causing Mom to slosh her light tan cup of Maxwell House, the only coffee she'd drink, heavily laced with at least an eighth of a cup of half and half and four teaspoons of sugar.

Sadly, Dad wasn't the only one becoming angered by the priest. Rumors swirled about how the man handled money, and parishioners left, heading to churches in Lansing or Owosso. Soon the congregation numbers dwindled enough where a new facility was not only not a necessity, it probably wasn't even a possibility.

In the summer of 2010 when it was apparent Dad's life was coming to an end, he wanted to discuss his final arrangements. A good friend still served on the Bethany Cemetery committee and said the chain-link fence surrounding the cemetery was a mess—a car had smashed into it and the damage had never been repaired.

"If anyone gives any sort of remembrance of me, what do you say we give it to the cemetery so they can build a new fence?" Dad asked.

My father died in the early morning hours of Saturday, July 31. Two days later, I traveled back home to the lone funeral home in Perry, since Morrice didn't have one, to make his arrangements. I asked the memorial envelopes be marked for St. Mary's Catholic Church and any checks be made out to the Bethany Cemetery fund so a new fence could be constructed. My father was a very beloved man and "any sort of remembrance" became a sizable amount of money. Friends and relatives were delighted they could do any little thing to honor Dad's wishes, and the donations poured in.

Perhaps it's all the trauma surrounding the memory, but I can't recall exactly how I learned Father Dick decided he would not honor Dad's request. I think I may have received a call from the same friend who told him the fence needed to be replaced. I do remember the gist of the message, though.

"Father doesn't want to put the memorial contributions toward a fence. He wants to buy fill dirt."

In my fury, I dashed off emails to all of my relatives, who in turn sent back lengthy letters of outraged indignation stressing their donations on behalf of such a wonderful person should *never* be used in such a disrespectful way. I stuffed them into an oversized envelope and mailed them to the governing diocese with my own furious, invective-filled note.

I never heard back from the diocese, but a couple weeks later I got a stern letter of reprimand from Father Dick. He rambled on and on and on about his "dismay" and "disappointment" and concluded with this, "Your father would be ashamed of you."

I don't drink whiskey very often anymore. I'm not the best human I can be when I do, and I gave up my heavy habit a few years ago.

But in 2010, it was still my beverage of choice, and I drank almost a pint that night. Then I called the church office to leave a message.

Obviously, I was drunk. I went into my walk-in closet so Jim wouldn't hear and let loose all my anger. In retrospect, perhaps I was also screaming at the boys who'd teased Dad so unmercifully he'd had to change schools as a child, the ticket takers who wouldn't let a poor boy into the movies because he only had script to offer, the church that wouldn't allow him and my mother to get married at the front altar, and the social services workers who wouldn't consider my parents' application to adopt because Mom wasn't Catholic. Perhaps I was even screaming a bit at myself and the times I'd selfishly resented having to put my own life aside to try to help my father through his waning days.

I'm not sure exactly what I said, though I am sure the very sweet St. Mary's receptionist named Cindy, whom my father really liked, probably got the message and likely had to hold the phone away from her ear. I *think* my rant went something like this:

"My father would never be disappointed in *me*. But let me tell you this you *jerk* [I may have said *asshole*], my father liked everyone, but he didn't like *you*. He loathed and despised *you*."

That was the end of it. Except, as I demanded, the church sent me back all of the money donated on Dad's behalf, and we sent it instead to my father's favorite charity, Leader Dog for the Blind in Rochester, Michigan.

A brick has now been placed there in honor of both my parents. It says, "In honor of Jim and Millie Eddington. For them, generosity was a way of life."

I know Father Dick was wrong. My father would not have been ashamed of me for sticking up for what was right. But he *would* have been dismayed and saddened I told his secret. He'd nobly and valiantly hidden his dislike of the man all those years, and I never saw him treat Father with anything but respect in person. I outed him after all the hard, frustrating work, and I will be forever sorry.

My parents are buried side by side at Bethany Cemetery. My mother's funeral was held on a blustery late November day in 2007 at the Perry funeral home and my father's was at St. Mary's on a hot early August day two and a half years later. We'd lucked out, and Father Dick was traveling when Dad died and a monsignor whom my father knew well and liked performed the ceremony.

Following each burial, we returned to the St. Mary's church basement where the kind guild women provided a comforting and aromatic warm chicken dinner in honor of my mother and a fresh-from-the-garden, vegetable-laden summer feast for my father.

Throughout the years, I've made the 230-mile round trip visit to my parents' graves almost every season to bring fresh flowers in the spring and summer or wreaths in the fall and winter. The few times when I've been unable to go, a cadre of friends and relatives have stepped in and often surprised me by making the visits to decorate the graves and say a prayer or two.

In January 2021, I had my second back surgery in fifteen months. My recovery, coupled with a frightening third or fourth spike of COVID-19 cases in Michigan in the spring kept me from traveling to Morrice. The first opportunity I had was in early July, just a week after Jim and I made our "up north" visit to Harrison to bury Ray in the Summerfield Township Cemetery. I put a pretty wreath near them and bowed my head as I said the Lord's Prayer. I always tell them a little something about what's going on in my life, and during that visit I said, "You won't *believe* the story I'm going to tell you."

Chapter 22

THE ANTI-FUNERAL

The day that was slated for Ray's *second* internment I decided to mimic my husband and dressed as nicely as I thought was appropriate for a country burial with only Jim, myself, and a cemetery sexton in attendance. I pulled on my favorite black jumpsuit, sandals, and small earrings. I grabbed an umbrella, as Michigan had been under the specter of torrential downpours for days. I worried about whether I should try to say something—a couple off-the-cuff remarks or an "I wish I'd met you, Ray." But it seemed too weird to imagine. I decided maybe I'd just recite the Lord's Prayer silently, my go-to graveside thing.

"Fair warning," I told Jim. "I'm planning on having a cocktail at lunch."

"Understood," he replied.

The rain disappeared as we drove, and the sun shone. Jim and I laughed and visited for the two-and-a-half-hour trip, stopping once at one of Michigan's omnipresent Wesco gas stations for a bathroom break and to buy some Vernors diet ginger ale. I also picked up a single cellophane-wrapped, peach-colored rose from inside the soft drink cooler.

"To leave for Ray," I told Jim. "It will die in a day out there, but I don't want to leave him with nothing."

We'd just passed the Harrison City Limits sign and were moments from swinging by Jean's house to pick up Ray's cremains when my dashboard lit up with an incoming call.

"Patti, it's Jean. I have some bad news," she said. "I can't find him."

We went to her house a few hours later after dropping off some flowers for Jaclyn and followed her directions to the cemetery. We easily located Ray's headstone, etched with the crane, and with its open hole . . . waiting. Jean was apologetic and sure he'd been in her closet but didn't seem confident he could be easily located. We visited with her for about fifteen minutes, then turned around and headed back home. We stopped at a roadside bar and grille in tiny Lake Station, where we both sat shaking our heads and I had my much anticipated cocktail.

"How are you . . . you know what? Never mind," Jim said.

"Honestly, at this point, I'm not even surprised," I told him.

Then we drove home and I put the little, wilting, peach-colored rose in a glass of water because I had no idea what else to do.

Chapter 23

MEXICAN BLOOD

....

Parent's View of Adoption
Although Mr. and Mrs. Eddington are very fond
of Patty, and have done an exceptional job of rais-
ing her, they are somewhat concerned about the
Mexican parentage of Patty. They fear that she
will have dark skin and it will be obvious that
she is Mexican. Mr. and Mrs. Eddington claim
that when the child was placed in their home they
were not aware that she had Mexican blood in
her and they found out about this through their
attorney. Worker tried to assure them that Patty's
skin would not become dark as she grew older, as
it is so fair and sensitive now.

Mr. and Mrs. Eddington seemed unduly con-
cerned also, about the fact that the child had relatives
living in the county and at one time they had taken
Patty to a school function and she had been recog-
nized by her two older sisters who were also there.
Mr. and Mrs. Eddington fear that the mother at
some time might interfere with the child.

*The Eddingtons expressed the desire that this
adoption not be completed within a year. They
would rather hold off a while until they could be
more sure of themselves.*

—Taken directly from Report of Investigation re: Patricia Ann
Eddington, (Mary Ann Ball), April 2, 1962. File no. 693—
(Mrs.) Barbara Trezise, Court Worker

....

In the month after I'd received my packet from the court, I
suffered over its contents. When Jim had asked, "You know
they loved you very much, right?" I told him "of course"
automatically because I knew—absolutely knew—it was true.

I thought about a time in either high school or college
when Mom and I were in some discussion about a topic
long-forgotten, and she said, "And of course I'd die for
you." Surely it is an emotion felt by all good mothers around
the globe, but it took me by surprise. I wasn't taken aback
because she *felt* it but rather because she *said* it. Until my
parents aged, maybe within a decade of their deaths, when we
began ending every conversation with "I love you" and every
in-person visit with long, emotion-filled hugs, such overt
proclamations of affection were rare enough, I probably
stared at her wide-eyed.

There wasn't one iota of doubt in my mind at the end
of *their* lives, my parents had loved me beyond measure.
The Report of Investigation sent to me by the court just had
me worried it might not have been the case at the *beginning*
of my life. The remark about my skin becoming dark was
upsetting. It just didn't make sense. I couldn't imagine my
parents always the epitome of class and such well-read and
intelligent people, making that abhorrent comment.

I didn't doubt they were concerned about me having relatives in the county, though. Reading my parents seemed "unduly concerned" about relatives living nearby and the mother interfering gave me pause. I'm not sure what I was thinking all those years, even after I learned the *first* time my birthday had been altered.

What I now realize is my mother would have tried to learn everything and anything about my biological family she could. I had only to look at what happened when I began dating for confirmation.

Being the only child of strict, Depression-era parents meant a lot of rules for me, including not dating until I was sixteen. I had thought it was old fashioned but knew it was useless to fight about it. Aside from the boy who'd been kicked off the bus for pulling the knife, it didn't seem like I'd have any takers in any case. For all my childhood expressions of love—kissing family friend Wayne Boughner in a tent and neighbor kid Larry Carbary in our basement when I was about eight—my ability to attract males slowed down immensely by the time I was a teenager.

But just about the time I turned sixteen, I grabbed the attention of a short, auburn-haired boy in my class, and he and his handsome cousin began driving back and forth down our road slowly until my dad stormed out to head them off by our mailbox.

I'd shared a few sips of putrid Annie Green Springs wine in the back of my friend Rex's car at a high school dance and tried unsuccessfully to flirt with an adorably chubby sophomore who told me his mom wouldn't let him go out with an older student who could drive. The fact I was seen as any kind of threat to his virginity was hysterical to me. It probably was just his way of letting me down easily. I saw him kissing a pretty classmate of mine named Jane near the school "cafetorium" within a couple weeks.

When Jim, who went to Owosso High School, called to ask me out after we met at the birthday party for Clara, I said yes immediately. I remembered he was cute and tall with a beard, but honestly it probably wouldn't have mattered. I'd had the magical sixteenth birthday a couple of months before, and I wanted to go on a real *date*.

"Where is Jim taking you?" Mom asked.

We'd planned a trip to East Lansing to go to the Michigan State University Planetarium (I'd later learn it was Jim's favorite place to take dates—nice and dark) but the weather report led his dad to nix our plan. We went to see a Disney movie in Owosso instead. I started to explain it to her, but it turned out her question was just a conversation starter.

"So, I drove by his house," she continued. "I think it's just fine."

This was long before the days of GPS directions, so Mom must have figured out his address and referenced an actual paper map to find the hidden side street where Jim's family lived.

Such tenacity of spirit and curiosity on her part is why I now realize my parents must *certainly* have had more information about my origins than I thought.

Reading the court document, I initially had a nagging fear they truly *were* concerned about raising a dark-skinned child in an almost completely homogenous white community. But . . . no. That entire section of the report just wasn't making sense to me, because my parents were no-nonsense people who wanted a child and adored me from the start. I did not believe melanin would mean a thing to them. I did, however, believe something wasn't adding up. And I thought I knew who could help me prove it.

Chapter 24

PEELING OFF THE PAPER

I called my cousin Pat again and spat out my questions nervously, ironically just as she was on her way to visit Aunt Dorothy's grave in February 2020, a few weeks after getting my adoption record packet in the mail.

Just six years older than me, Aunt Dorothy's youngest daughter would have been only about nine as my adoption was in its final stages. I wasn't sure she'd have an accurate memory of what I needed to know, but I had to try.

"So, brace yourself," I told her. "What Mom and Dad told the court worker was they wanted to wait to finalize the adoption to make sure . . . my skin didn't turn dark."

There was a long silence.

"Oh, my God. Okay. Well, look, your parents loved you. You know it. We *all* know it," she said deliberately, almost exactly as Jim had. "And . . . that does not sound like them at all."

"Of course I do, and no it doesn't, and here's what I think," I said.

I told Pat I believed my parents had been lying to the court, that I was sure they'd *always* known about my heritage, and it would *never* have mattered to them. I believed *they* didn't have an issue but knew there was something going on in their lives that might cause the probate court to be concerned about letting me stay with them and they were desperately trying to buy time.

"That has to be it," she replied. "Let me look through some of Mom's papers when I get home. I'll call you back."

Just six years earlier, I'd composed Aunt Dorothy's eulogy in my head during a three-hour car ride from St. Joseph Mercy Hospital in Ann Arbor back home to Spring Lake. The rumors of her death were premature, but not by much, and she'd already asked Pat to have my cousin Ted and I speak at her funeral. After years living on one deadline or another, I'd learned I didn't have to decide what to write only when sitting in front of a screen. I'd composed some of my best ledes—the beginning paragraph of an article— while in the shower or driving.

I knew I wanted to tell the story about playing on the swing set in sixth grade when the little girl told me her mother said she shouldn't play with me since I didn't live with my "real" family. And I wanted to talk about what "real" meant because I'd never have a "real-er" relative than Aunt Dorothy, my beloved godmother.

I thought back to a Saturday night decades earlier in an Ann Arbor hotel room, getting ready to go to a surprise thirtieth birthday party for Kristen and chatting on the phone with Aunt Dorothy, who was undergoing major back surgery two days later. It was the first of two such procedures, neither of which would do much toward repairing her crumbling spine.

"What are you doing talking to me? I'm fine. You just go have a great time," she said.

It was a comment representative of my loving, selfless aunt who always wanted everyone *else* to be okay. Her life read like the story line of a soap opera, yet she greeted each challenge with, "I just look around. There is *always* someone worse off than me."

I was a young girl when Mom whispered to me, even though we were alone, that Aunt Dorothy had gotten pregnant at seventeen and had to leave high school. It was the early 1940s, and the shame on the Block family was heavy.

Her strict German parents asked her to leave home, so she married the baby's father, Jim Lyon, and moved in with her older sister, Esther (younger than my mother), and Esther's husband, Chester. Esther and Chester were also persona non grata with the family, since Chet was Armenian. My Catholic father also struggled to win over his staunch Protestant in-laws for some time.

"Then, one Sunday I was sitting in the living room waiting for your mother, and her father was reading his paper, as usual. He sighed, lowered the paper, and said reluctantly, 'Do you want a beer?' And I knew I was in," Dad told me.

Dorothy and Jim had their baby, Penny, followed shortly after with another daughter, Sandy, and eventually Pat, raising them in a small, farm-style house situated on a huge double lot in Garden City. If things had settled down and life had gotten a bit easier for my aunt, it wasn't long-lived.

I have only vague memories of Anna Block, my maternal grandmother, but always remember the story I was told about the night she died.

My parents had spent the day visiting her in her hospital bed in Detroit, where she'd languished with breast cancer for several months. They'd driven the two hours back home to Morrice—I'm not sure who had been caring for me—and had just walked in the door when the phone rang with the news she had passed away.

That was November 27, 1962. On December 5, only eight days later, Aunt Dorothy and Uncle Jim's teenage pregnancy baby, Penny, got married at nineteen and only a few weeks later, on January 20, just nine days after his forty-second birthday, Uncle Jim dropped dead of a cerebral brain hemorrhage at the kitchen table, leaving my thirty-seven-year-old aunt a widow with two young daughters still at home.

A high school dropout who'd never had a job, with no savings and living off social security benefits, Aunt Dorothy began investigating how to earn her GED. She happened into a secretarial position. She had no experience, just a warm, kind personality and a desperate need to work to help her little family survive.

My earliest memories of my beloved aunt are in the mid-to-late 1960s. A tall, slender, black-haired beauty in a mini-skirt and towering bouffant hairdo, she drank Pepsi almost non-stop, sat lotus style on the living room floor while the other adults sat primly on our streamlined mid-century modern couch, and taught me how to do the twist. I thought she was a goddess and possibly the coolest woman in the world.

Aunt Dorothy eventually met her second husband, a quiet, Dean Martin lookalike (down to the cigarette and cocktail in his hand) named Bob and married him when I was thirteen. They moved to a penthouse apartment, which featured not only a spiral staircase but a rain lamp in the bedroom—the height of elegance in my prepubescent world. Pat still has the incredible, beloved lamp in her dining room in memory of her mother.

When I was a poor college student at MSU and keeping the thermostat set low to save money, Aunt Dorothy sent me a care package filled with candy, flannel footie pajamas, and a card saying how much she loved me. She told me I was pretty, and one day I would be a great writer. She was absolutely everything a godmother should be.

As she aged and it became apparent her back surgeries had failed, Aunt Dorothy relied more on a walker, eventually able to stand at no more than a forty-five-degree angle. She watched as her husband, Bob, dwindled away, suffering first from years of unrelenting cluster headaches and then cancer. Toward the end, he begged her to help him end his life.

"I told him I couldn't," she told me sadly but matter-of-factly. "I just couldn't. It wasn't right."

Even at the end of her own life, her body horrifically bent and fragile, I never heard her ask for pity.

"I've been so lucky," she'd say. "I know when I go out in public people look at me strangely. I know how I look. But so many people have a harder time. I don't feel sorry for myself."

On Labor Day weekend 2013, a week before her final trip to the hospital, we all gathered at The Inn at St. John in Plymouth, a former provincial seminary, which had been converted into a beautiful hotel and event venue, to celebrate the marriage of Pat's son, Gregory. The sanctuary was developed for seminary students, so the nave was designed with the pews facing the center aisle. As a cellist played the beautiful song "The Prayer," Gregory escorted his grandmother up the aisle to her seat. She beamed the entire way, smiling and acknowledging her family and friends.

And I finally *completely* believed there are other ways to be a queen besides winning a pageant.

Within ten days, our darling would be hospitalized and make the request regarding her eulogy.

Gathered around her bedside on her final day, we took turns holding her hands and reminiscing. As I kissed her cheek, she mumbled something softly.

"I'm sorry, Aunt Dorothy. I didn't quite hear you," I said, leaning in closer.

"Mumble, mumble."

"I'm so sorry. Still not sure," I said, panic rising. My sweet aunt was making one last request of me. A request I'd never be able to fulfill because I was too stupid to understand what she was asking.

Her eyes flew open, caught mine, and she enunciated perfectly and precisely this time. "Pepsi!"

I flew down to the lobby and found a can in a pop machine in a hallway. The same grandson who'd walked her down the aisle, who ironically worked for Coca Cola, gave her small sips of her favorite soda and she died shortly after.

Molly and I emerged from the hospital exhausted but knew Pat would soon have a house full of relatives. We dashed through the local big box grocery store, picking up cheese, wine, and snacks, then did our best to set up what would turn out to be a relieved and somewhat drunken, cathartic wake on the back patio of Pat's home as the sun set on the last day of our sweetheart's life.

The stories we told were the same ones we'd told over and over through the years but comforting to us as we began to navigate our grief over the immense loss.

"And then there was the time Rob set fire to her house," someone began, as they always did, regaling us all yet again with the time our naughty cousin, Uncle Bill's second oldest, played with matches at Aunt Dorothy's home. He had ignited a blaze, which necessitated several fire engines.

Aunt Dorothy had simply said, "I wanted to remodel anyway."

"And what about the time Patti peeled off her bedroom wallpaper?" someone else added, laughing.

And it was *that story*, when I remembered it in February 2020, which was my *aha* moment.

It wasn't because I'd peeled off the wallpaper—it was the reason I had access to the wallpaper in the first place. My adoption wasn't even finalized, but my parents had sent me to live with Aunt Dorothy. And they hadn't notified the court.

Chapter 25

SALLY SQUIRREL
GETS A NEW HAT

If only life was like a movie and there was a soundtrack to alert you to sudden danger, tell you you'd be a complete idiot to go down those basement steps, or warn you to not get into the creepy car. Or maybe it would make you stop, tilt your head, and take notice when someone tells you a bit of information you will need one day. It would have been nice if there would be a lilting little melody every time to tell me, "Hey, listen up. You'll *want* to know this."

The story is so familiar it is unclear if I have those misty memories myself or if I only *think* I recall what happened.

It was obviously a touchstone in my mother's life, and she told the tale often. I was very young but I still recall being sent to school with Pat, who must have been in about third grade. Her classmates treated me like a pet, putting me in the teacher's chair and spinning me around when she left the room for a moment. I remember the fear I'd done something wrong and would be in trouble when she clickety-clacked back into the room in her high heels. I'm sure I don't remember being tucked into Aunt Dorothy's bed for a nap and systematically working at a loose piece of wallpaper until I'd collected quite a pile of torn pieces on the bed beside me, but the story was so much a part of family legend, it *seems* familiar.

I *do* recall my favorite story at the time, though— *Sally Squirrel Gets a New Hat.* It was a small, paperboard book describing the trials of little Sally Squirrel who was vain and proud and something of a braggart because of her fancy new chapeau. She boasted about it to all her woodland friends only to have it blow away one windy day. Ultimately, she found an oak leaf to tie under her chin as a bonnet and realized, though less fancy, it was just as lovely and worked just as well. It was a cute story for toddlers, which also came with a moral.

"Dorothy was just amazed you could already read," my mother told me repeatedly through the years. "She said you'd read the book over and over and over to her. She never realized you had memorized the words and when to turn the pages."

Being so young, I obviously didn't understand my poor aunt had only recently lost both her mother and her husband and was probably struggling to keep dinner on the table for her daughters. She must have worried constantly about money and how she might possibly afford new wallpaper for her bedroom.

It certainly doesn't seem like an opportune time for my parents to send me to stay with her, and frankly it seems totally out of character for such otherwise thoughtful people. Pat has reminded me often that when her father died at the kitchen table and the call went out to relatives, Mom and Dad, though they lived more than an hour away, were the first people to make it to Aunt Dorothy's side.

Normally, they would be the last to impose in such a

way and leave such a young child with someone who was enduring so much. But they must have felt they had no other choice. They needed somewhere for me to stay since my mother was undergoing surgery. She'd been diagnosed with breast cancer.

Aunt Dorothy documented the date of Mom's surgery on a little piece of paper listing her family medical history. It was the scrap of paper Pat found after searching through boxes of her mother's belongings the day I made the "brace yourself" call.

Unlike my birthdates, my mother's description of her breast cancer diagnosis was one story she told me that never changed throughout the years. "We were in the process of moving forward with the adoption when I found a lump in my breast. We didn't know what to do. If something happened to me, Daddy would have been left all alone with a little girl to raise."

She visited three different doctors, convinced with her family history—besides her mother, her sister Esther and brother Bill would eventually also be diagnosed with breast cancer—she had something to worry about. Three times she was told it was a cyst.

Then one night she dreamed her dead mother sat down beside her and told her she needed to go to one more physician.

"Try one more time," she said her mother told her. "You *must* try one more time."

Since her mother hadn't died until November 1962, the dream obviously happened afterward, which means three times Mom made appointments, three times attended appointments, and three times been told she had nothing to worry about before her mother's nocturnal visit. It was a process that dragged on for months and no doubt was taking place in April of that year when the court worker Barbara Trezise wrote, "The Eddingtons expressed the desire that this adoption not be completed within a year. They would rather hold off until they could be more sure of themselves."

While I stayed with Aunt Dorothy and recited *Sally Squirrel*, Mom underwent a radical, unilateral mastectomy. In 1963, the process was extreme and disfiguring. The surgeons took not only her right breast but all the lymph nodes in the area, including under her arm. She was forty-seven when she had the surgery, and she lived to be ninety-one. For the rest of her more than forty-four years, she was unable to lift her right arm above her head.

Being the most pragmatic of humans, she never complained about her limited range of motion or even of going through life with one breast. Breast reconstruction wasn't widely performed then, and even if it had been, Mom wouldn't have opted in. Instead, she purchased a not very life-like, heavy prosthesis to try to even herself up. The prosthesis was a large, pale, squishy, pear-shaped orb she affixed with large safety pins into her bra anytime she left home. Around the house, wearing the prosthesis was determined by whether it was a humid day or time for the orb to be washed and set out to dry on the bathroom vanity. Some of my most vivid memories of Mom in my childhood involve her speeding along on her beloved John Deere riding lawnmower—nobody else except Dad was allowed on it and even that was rare—wearing a homemade purple halter top, her curly blond hair and one breast bouncing.

"It was my breast or my life, and it wasn't even a close contest," she told me.

Her c'est la vie attitude was no doubt the right one, and when I was a small child, she would sing to me the Doris Day tune "Que Sera, Sera" as she went about her housework. But I worried when I was a teenager and she volunteered for an American Cancer Society program called Reach to Recovery. She visited recent mastectomy patients at the hospital, showed them exercises, and listened to their fears. I realized by this time some women would definitely mourn the loss of a breast, and I worried about her response to them since she was so matter-of-fact about her loss and grief.

"Mom, what do you do if they cry?" I asked, afraid she'd say she'd give them a stern lecture about self-pity and gratitude.

"Oh," she said. "It happens. And, when it happens . . . I just hold their hand."

Chapter 26

MY THEORY

....

Re: Mary Ann Ball
File No. 693
2.4.63
I visited the Eddington Home and found that
Mary Ann is doing very well in the home. She is a
very attractive girl and Mrs. Eddington remarks
she appears to be above normal in intelligence and
is very responsive and bright. The Eddingtons
expressed that they are very happy with Mary
Ann, and they have no negative feelings regarding
Mary Ann's paternal blood.

—Taken directly from the Report of Investigation re: Patricia
Ann Eddington, (Mary Ann Ball), February 4 1963. File No.
693—(Thomas R. Wood Court Worker)

....

There is absolutely no mention in the adoption paperwork about my mother's health. She had surgery just a month after Thomas Wood visited and noted my parents had "no negative feelings regarding Mary Ann's paternal blood."

Mr. Wood apparently took over for court worker Barbara Trezise. I found it poignant that the woman who seemed to have tried so desperately to convince my parents it would be just fine to carry on with my adoption (*Worker tried to to assure them Patty's skin would not become dark as she grew older*) might not have ever known the real reason for their reticence—my mother's health.

Researching her online, I discovered she had been married to Doug Trezise, a former mayor of Owosso, who eventually became a Michigan legislator. The couple had six children, including two sets of twins, and she died at seventy-nine on July 11, 2007; ironically that day was my mother's last birthday. She'd turned ninety-one, and we'd given her a little surprise celebration.

I found a contact email and reached out to Barbara's son, Doug, who told me he couldn't tell me much about his mother's years with the court, but he did know why she wasn't able to do the follow-up visit with my parents. She'd been pregnant with him and stayed home for several years before going back to work. I wonder if she ever thought about our family again.

I've always been fascinated by the Baader-Meinhof phenomenon, which occurs when you notice something new—at least new to you—and then suddenly you notice it *everywhere*. It typically happens to me when I've purchased a new make of car, like my Ford Flex, and then it seems like just about the only model of car I see on the road is the Flex. That's kind of how it is with adoption; it seems like almost everyone has a story.

One adoptive mother I know is the woman who was my fifth-grade teacher, Candy Koga Zann. Candy burst into Morrice Elementary school like a petite, blond, ray of sunshine—the most beautiful, fun, and creative teacher I'm sure the little town had ever known. A recent Michigan

State graduate, she taught our ragtag bunch of hellions about nature and nutrition. She took us for walks and pointed out species of wildlife, helped us create dolls, and taught us to sing a raucous, knee-slapping, Hawaiian song, "Going on a Buta Hunt."

On Cinco de Mayo, she had us bring in ingredients so we could make lunch—the first taco I'd ever eaten. And when after just one year teaching in our small town she moved to Hawaii, she held an auction allowing us to bid with toy money on beloved items from her desk and classroom to take with us to remember our incredible year. I got a ball of yellow yarn, and it was a treasured possession. She was *that* teacher, the one who is right there beside you, whispering in your ear for the rest of your life.

Candy came back to visit Morrice once or twice and gathered as many students in our class as she could for a visit. She and her husband had adopted two daughters, and for a long time I received a Christmas card with a photo of her lovely family. We lost touch over the decades, but then a few years ago I tracked her down to find she was back in Michigan. We got together for lunch and now talk regularly. She'd adopted her daughters in 1975 and 1981.

"Do you think my parents might have intentionally not notified the court of my mother's health issues, worrying it might make a difference?" I asked her.

"Well, I can tell you this," Candy said. "When we went through the process, our health was of utmost importance to the powers that be."

Even a decade and more *after* Mom and Dad adopted me, the health of the adoptive parents, at least in some parts of the United States, was of the *utmost* importance. And I'm sure my parents knew it.

Here's my theory: We know Mom visited four physicians before getting the breast cancer diagnosis. Yet while the court worker's notes (I am always happy to point out to Jim) mention I was "attractive," "responsive," and "bright," they don't touch on any type of potential roadblocks to pushing forward with the adoption. I believe Mom's illness wasn't mentioned in any court paperwork because she and Dad decided it *couldn't* be. While she was likely fighting for a diagnosis for over a year—even as her mother lay dying of the same disease that likely presented its own set of difficulties and stressors—it *never* came up with the officials at probate court. I believe my parents weighed the decision and decided in the early 1960s it would be better to be considered racist by the few court workers who would see the report than to let them know Mom was sick.

My bet is they decided to play for time, saying they were concerned my skin might turn dark and they'd like to hold off on finalizing my adoption. They still couldn't be sure of the outcome of the surgery she would have of course, but they had a plan and they had come through so much already. When Mom told me the story of her breast cancer diagnosis just as they were getting ready to adopt me, she said my aunt Liz, Dad's older sister, told her to put her worries aside and put her faith in a higher power.

"Patti could be adopted by younger, completely healthy parents and they could be in an accident. There are never guarantees. It will be okay," Aunt Liz told her.

Mom and Dad must have decided to take a huge leap of faith and as the court worker wrote, ". . . expressed that they are very happy with Mary Ann."

Chapter 27

THE THING ABOUT
THE TRUTH, REDUX

I will never know the absolute truth about why a judge made a decision that ultimately placed me with Millie and Jim and not Jane and Cecil.

When I first heard the gut-wrenching "but then we never saw you again" story from Aunt Eva and investigated the why, I thought I probably *did* know. As a journalist, I was trained to never *assume*. But sadly, I assumed the hell out of it. I imagined a judge in the early 1960s in rural mid-Michigan might not like the idea of placing me, with my light-colored, fair, and sensitive skin, with a mixed-race couple. Since he was very likely deceased, there wouldn't be a way to find out the truth in any case. Still, as I neared the end of telling this story, a low-level feeling of guilt that I should at least *try* to find out what happened finally got me. Also, I had the judge's name and the ability to do a Google search. As I suspected I would, I found his obituary. It said the former judge died at age ninety-two. He'd served in the Navy during World War II and later graduated from Knox College in Illinois and the University of Michigan

Law School. A democrat, he had an unsuccessful run for prosecuting attorney in 1954 but was elected as a probate court judge in 1956.

The obit also stated Judge Clark Shanahan returned to private practice following his two terms as a probate judge and had a lengthy and distinguished career in which he was instrumental in vital community mental health legislation and passionate about cases involving children. He was especially proud of helping expand the statute of limitations for victims of child sexual abuse. He sounded like a solid, well-intentioned, stand-up guy; a man I would have liked.

A couple things about his obituary especially stood out. The first thing was his obvious youth. He was born in 1928, so he was only twenty-eight years old when he became a judge and a mere thirty-two when he terminated Lois's parental rights over me and my four older siblings. The termination order he signed indicated all "interested" parties had been notified, listing Lois and her parents, Oliver and Dorothea. The biological fathers of us weren't even mentioned, but two other people were: Aunt Jane and her husband, Cecil. They were apparently "interested parties" because of their desire to adopt me.

I'd assumed as a judge he would have been *at least* middle aged in the early 1960s and probably long since deceased. But his obituary was from April 2020. He died at ninety-two, just a few weeks after I received my court documents. Had I only been a bit quicker, perhaps I could have spoken with him.

I did speak to one of his children, though. The obituary listed five biological offspring, the youngest being Susan, recently retired from a long career in education and still living in Owosso. I tracked her down and—reminiscent of my note to Jean Parker—sent off a long message to her via Facebook.

"Thank you for speaking with me," I told her when she told me I could call her just a few days later. "I'm not sure what *I* would have said had I gotten that kind of message."

Susan was warm, welcoming, and good-natured, and while I hesitated to tell her some parts of my story and my initial worries—I was concerned at the heart of the matter there was racism—I did finally tell it all to her, and she listened attentively. Rather than act with indignation, she was truly thoughtful in her response.

"I understand why you might think that but . . . no," she said. "That doesn't sound like him at all."

Concerned because she didn't want to make her father appear like a "some of my best friends are Black people" kind of guy, she also thought it was important for me to know both of her parents were liberal in an era and a location where it wasn't necessarily popular. They made it a point to discuss incidents with racial overtones and discrimination with their children. She said her dad was known for his kindness, fairness, and compassion. He even adopted a moratorium on spanking his children because he'd seen so many cases of child abuse.

"He never wanted a hand raised to a child," she told me. "I wish my father could have talked with you. I know he would have enjoyed that."

Obviously, there are other reasons Judge Shanahan may have been averse to allowing Jane and Cecil to follow through with adopting me. I would have been raised in the same small city where my biological mother lived and where my siblings were still being shuffled around in the foster care system. And I'd learned Jane and Ray were the closest of siblings. In an era before open adoptions, it might have been frowned upon to have a biological father in regular contact with his offspring.

Maybe there was some other reason, but I will never know. I will never know what my life would have been like or who I would have turned out to be. I've mused about it with Jim, reminding him if things had turned out differently, I would have gone to the same high school he did.

"I wonder if, in such a large school, Jim Moore and Mary Ann Lopez would have even crossed paths?"

And my husband, being my wonderful rose-colored glasses fan of fans, says each time, "Of course we would have. I would have found you. Have you *seen* you?"

The answer to his question is no.

I never saw me and could not *truly* see me until I understood everything I could possibly understand of my history. I had to learn about all my families, my many birthdays, and the incredible luck or fate or serendipity that put me in the arms of Millie and Jim. I needed to know that my parents had been able to push past their fear and believe my mother would survive so they could finally achieve their dream of being parents.

They are very happy with Mary Ann.

There have certainly been difficult and unsettling moments in the journey since I visited the courthouse that blustery January day and many times when I wondered if I should have opened such a Pandora's box. But ultimately, I'm glad I finally know some of this long, complicated, heartbreaking but, in the end, uplifting story. Because I can finally appreciate this much: it is mine.

Chapter 28

LOSING AUNT EVA

I'm not a great public speaker. My voice shakes; my throat goes dry. I do it sometimes, but whenever I take my seat afterward, my vision is wavy and my pulse races.

But I felt drawn to do it one unseasonably warm early November day in 2022. I made my way to the podium in front of an overflowing funeral home chapel filled with sniffling women and men who had gathered to pay homage and say goodbye to one of the kindest women any of us had ever, or would ever, know.

So many people in the room were united in the knowledge that every time their birthdays came around, they would get a call from her.

"Hello, honey. It's Aunt Eva Lopez Lytle." And then she'd sing the birthday song.

I had five years of Aunt Eva—the young woman holding me in the first photo I now have of little Mary Ann Lopez—calling me on October 19. The first four times she said the exact same thing in her excitable little voice, her lilting cadence.

"Hello, honey! It's Aunt Eva Lopez Lytle! I know it's not the day *you* celebrate. But to *me*, it's your birthday!" And then she'd sing me the birthday song.

She did it a fifth time on October 19, 2022, as well, but the cheery little voice was gone. She sang to me, but she was sobbing. I believe she knew it would be the last time she would ever wish me a happy birthday. It was maybe the last time she would wish anyone a happy birthday, actually, and sitting back down at the funeral home, wavy vision, dry throat, I was pissed off and tried to remind myself I'd done okay. I'd paid tribute to our funny, four-foot-nothing imp with the child-sized feet and the tender heart, who loved Elvis Presley and a bizarre cocktail made with Fireball and cream soda.

I was angry Aunt Eva died, because I believed it was unnecessary and certainly before her time. And the weight of my anger fell directly on her "boyfriend" Ted, right where it belonged, in my opinion.

The night before her funeral, Jim gave me a serious look and said, "I wish I could come with you. Remember just put your nose in the air and walk right by him. Don't engage." Jim knows all about my temper. He knew I'd want to engage. He also knew I'd regret it.

"I won't," I promised him. "I've thought of what I will say if I have to talk to him and I'm just going to say, 'Ted, I'm sorry for your loss. At least Aunt Eva is out of her *agony*.'"

Agony, not *pain*. The semantics are important because her *agony* was avoidable.

I didn't say it, though. Ted approached me as I visited with biological family members I'd only met a few times. He was pale, shaky, and bleary eyed. *Maybe*, I thought, *maybe he finally understands she didn't need to die, not now, not in this way. Maybe he understands he played a role, a big role, in it.*

"Patti," he said, voice cracking with emotion, tears in his eyes.

"Ted," I said. "I'm sorry for your loss. At least Aunt Eva is out of her . . . pain."

I chickened out, obviously. Some force, God or common sense or basic human kindness, kicked in and I checked myself.

Thank goodness for small moments of grace because maybe five minutes after I got up and spoke about my love for that dear elfin princess . . . Ted collapsed. Not just a little fainting spell, but a "stop-the-funeral, everybody step to the side, call 911, airlift Ted to a Level One trauma center an hour away because he is probably going to die" collapsed. It turned out his pale, shaky countenance was the product of an abdominal aortic aneurysm and not grief.

I drove the two hours home after the funeral in disbelief, calling Molly, Jim, and my friends Cathy, Diane, and of course Kristen, saying abdominal aortic aneurysm but *thinking* the cause of Ted's collapse was the result of something much more cosmic—karma.

After I had met Aunt Eva at the quinceañera in 2018, and she told me the wrenching "and then we never saw you again" story, I kept in touch with her and her sister, my aunt Sandy. I'd send cards and little gifts for all occasions—Halloween, Valentine's, birthdays, Christmas—and I made the cross-state trip to visit whenever I could.

Shortly after I met her, Aunt Eva—who had been living with Terri, the cousin I first talked to through Ancestry.com—got her own apartment in a lovely, former elementary school, which was remodeled and used for low-income, senior citizen housing. Her connection to her relatives was strong, and she was always out with someone having fun, going shopping, spending time with family members, sometimes at the Rainbow Bar, the dive Ray frequented.

I tried calling her once, and after hours of not getting any answer, checked in with Terri.

"She's probably just at her boyfriend Ted's place," Terri said.

We initially all thought it was sweet and dear she'd found a love interest in her apartment building when she was seventy-four, having lost her devoted husband, Bud, years before.

But sitting around Aunt Eva's kitchen table visiting with several cousins one summer day, Ted began expressing his opinion on, well, everything. And two things became obvious: I thought he was an idiot and I wasn't the only one.

Listening to his harebrained medical philosophies—at the time I thought they were *only* harebrained because I didn't know one day they would become dangerous—I had to stop myself from telling him he was wrong. It was killing me, though. Luckily, one of Aunt Sandy's daughters stepped in, looked him straight in the eye after his lengthy diatribe against Western medicine, which ended with "and that's the truth," and said firmly, "No. It is not."

I love that cousin.

A day or so before Christmas Eve that year, Terri called me, frantic. "Have you heard from Aunt Eva, by any chance?" she asked. "Because we can't find her."

They did eventually find her living with Ted in a trailer in the woods in northern Michigan. They'd both left their apartments, apparently without notifying the landlord, and left the medicine prescribed for Aunt Eva's heart condition sitting in its white paper bag at the drugstore in Owosso as well. Ted didn't believe in heart medicine. He was going to cure her congestive heart failure and A-fib with vitamins. Drugstore staff grew concerned the vital prescription hadn't been picked up and alerted her family.

Aunt Eva and Ted stayed up north for maybe a year, a period where she landed in the hospital several times for painful swelling in her feet, eventually even having surgery. I sent cards, chicken noodle soup, and chocolate chip cookies from a company, which packaged the delicious little gifts of love with a pretty soup ladle.

Aunt Eva would call me to thank me and tell me all the great things Ted was doing for her.

"He bought me some socks."

"He's going to buy me a bed because, honey, we're not married yet you know. We can't sleep in the same bed."

"I wonder where she *has* been sleeping," one cousin worried.

Any time I visited with my aunt, she told me more stories about my early life I hadn't known. She told me it was her mother who gave Aunt Jane a few dollars to buy me the pretty, fluffy dress to wear to the courthouse the day Aunt Jane said, "When we come home, Mary Ann will be ours forever and ever." It was a sweet story tempered by the one where her mother had also tried to hide her away from experiences familiar to other children her age.

"She thought I was slow. She didn't really take me many places," she said.

It was a refrain I would hear repeatedly from some family members that perhaps Aunt Eva was on the autism spectrum. It had never been diagnosed because it probably wouldn't have been in a little girl born into a poor, migrant family working in the sugar beet fields and living in The Colony in the 1940s.

But Aunt Eva was blessed with an abundance of love— both in the giving and in the getting—from her large *familia* and she and Ted eventually did move back to Owosso to a much less lovely apartment than before on the second floor of a different subsidized housing building. The second floor was very difficult for Aunt Eva. There was no elevator, and the dozen or so steps to the top became more and more challenging and exhausting the longer she was off her prescribed medications.

The summer of 2022 was fraught with health scares and trauma for both Aunt Eva and the family who loved her. She was hospitalized with severe edema in her tiny feet and ankles but signed herself out after a physician threatened Ted with a restraining order. I'm not sure why the doctor became so angry, but I have some theories. Maybe Ted called her a "quack" and an "idiot" to her face, as he told me she was, or perhaps the doctor was simply trying to save Aunt Eva's life.

I've lost track of everything that happened because it was a lot. There was an early stay in a rehab center as well. Once again, Aunt Eva signed herself out after just a couple days. Ted bought an old car, somehow, and transported her to Ann Arbor to see a natural healer. They didn't have an appointment, and the healer didn't have the time to see her, so back home they went.

"They wouldn't even help her," Ted said.

"They didn't even help me," Aunt Eva seconded.

Hospitals don't love it when you sign yourself out against medical advice and neither did rehab centers. Ted and Eva were running out of options.

One early Saturday morning in August, I got a call from Ted asking if I was coming to Owosso that day.

"I'd planned on it, but I told Aunt Eva I would postpone until next week because it is supposed to be such bad weather," I replied. I'd hoped to take her out to lunch and to also drive by the house where I first lived with her, Jane, and Cecil when they'd hoped to adopt me. With her health issues, I thought I should make time to fit it in sooner rather than later.

"Here, you talk to her," he said.

Aunt Eva came to the phone in tears, telling me she was sick, couldn't sleep, it was very painful to urinate, and she was just standing in the living room crying all night. I asked her to call 911 or go back to the hospital.

"Those doctors never help me. They don't do anything to help me, honey," she said. Her extremities were so swollen she told me she was digging at her ankles with her fingernails and was bleeding.

"I get so anxious, honey," she said.

"I'll be there this afternoon," I said.

Jim insisted on joining me, something I was initially opposed to since my bright, practical husband with the scientific mind had not met Ted and I knew it wouldn't be a pleasurable experience. We took off through the rain and wind, picking up some sunflowers and her favorite cod and french fry lunch from a little Owosso diner called Greg and Lou's. We also grabbed a stethoscope and pulse oximeter from the clinic and some Neosporin to put on her wounds until we could get her to the hospital, because it sounded like she *needed* to be back in the hospital.

But we couldn't get her to go back to the hospital. Aunt Eva was buying into the disdain and distrust for the medical community Ted sprinkled liberally into every conversation.

The discussion that afternoon was agonizingly circuitous. Doctors weren't helping. Nobody was helping. They'd gone to the herbal specialist and healer in Ann Arbor, and he wouldn't help them, either. She was in great pain, and she was so anxious she would dig at her grotesquely swollen ankles and calves, which were indeed covered in oozing, blood-crusted sores.

Jim, who as a veterinarian is pretty accustomed to gross, couldn't suppress a gasp when he saw them.

"I kept thinking if only there was something Patti could do," Aunt Eva said, as she cried.

It was what I'd been worried about. She focused all her hopes on me—the long-lost Mary Ann—and I would be added to the lengthy list of those who "didn't help."

After her beloved husband Bud had died in the early 1990s, Aunt Eva was cared for beautifully by her nieces, nephews, and other family members. She was widely adored and made to feel extra-special.

Then Ted came into the picture, filling her ears with rubbish. She stopped taking her medicines, and when two nieces stepped in and spoke their mind to her about him, he apparently convinced her it was actually the relatives who were the bad guys. A few of us tried to keep open the lines of communication with her, and even though it irritated me beyond measure, with him as well. I'd just found her. I didn't want to lose her.

"Aunt Eva, I'm no expert," I told her that August day. "I don't have any special potions or a magic pony. Your oxygen level is at ninety. If you were in the hospital, they would probably put you on supplemental oxygen. The Neosporin might offer a little relief for your poor feet, but it won't cure the issue."

Never mind, though. Ted was going to cure her. When we asked if she was taking her heart medicine, he waved his hand to a huge cabinet in the corner of the tiny dining area. It was filled with bottles and jars—elixirs of false hope.

"All we need to do is get her heart working better," he said and told us he'd sent away for some special tree bark he would boil with milk.

I've only seen the look Jim gets when he'd like to punch someone a couple of times in my life, but I saw it that day.

We explained we believe in treating things as naturally as possible, as well. Eating well, vitamins, fruits and vegetables, and exercise.

"But there are some things that have to be treated medically, Aunt Eva," my dear husband said, focusing on her instead of Ted.

"Quacks," Ted chirped. "Quacks. Quacks. Quacks."

"They never do anything to help me, honey," Aunt Eva said.

We sadly gave up and went home.

In late September, Ted called me to say she'd been taken to yet another rehab place in Durand a few miles from Owosso. I told him I would go to see her the next day, and he was very grateful.

"You know, Patti, I never realized if your heart isn't doing well, it really affects a lot of things," he mused.

No kidding, you dimwit, was what I *wanted* to say. But I didn't.

Instead, I agreed to go more than an hour out of my way on a day that would already include a six hour-round trip to pick him up and take him to see her. He'd sold their car for some reason and had no transportation.

I was restless all night. I didn't want to take Ted. I didn't even want him in my car. I felt I'd been complicit in throwing my dear aunt into the maw of an ignorant lion who had already allowed her to live in much discomfort based on idiocy and would ultimately be the cause of her demise.

I texted him the next day and told him I couldn't help him. I lied about the reason, and for the first time in my life, I felt justified in a blatant lie.

We had such a nice visit in the rehab center. Aunt Eva told me she was feeling much better, and we talked for two hours about her younger years. She told me stories I'd never heard about her youth and reiterated all the same old tales as well.

"Ray said, 'Eva . . . one day you will find Mary Ann. You will *find* her!'"

She also told me she was ready to die.

"Ted doesn't want me to go, but I told him I'm ready," she said.

I told her, "I don't think it is your time. Yes, you have heart issues, but they are treatable if you stay put and follow the plan so you can feel better."

"I'm ready," she said.

"Okay," I said. "Are you afraid?"

She drew herself up and set her tiny chin. "I am *not* afraid."

The next day, Ted sent me a photo of the autumn planter filled with flowers I'd taken her, which said Grateful in a pretty script on the side. It sat on their kitchen counter. She had checked herself out the day after my visit.

She died less than a month later, and then Ted collapsed. I confess I had little sympathy.

"I hope after they airlifted him, they didn't treat him with *Western* medicine," I texted a few people. "If only he were conscious, perhaps he could advise those quack doctors to let him sip the fluid of the left nut of the youngest yak on the furthermost side of the shortest mountain in Peru so he can be cured."

I acted like a jerk, frankly, and I'm sure Aunt Eva wouldn't approve.

What *has* helped me is something a cousin told me at the funeral. Ted, who introduced himself to all as Aunt Eva's fiancé, brought a dress for her to be laid to rest. Someone had given it to her to wear at their eventual wedding, a wedding Aunt Eva talked about at times but somehow never made plans to carry out. The dress was a bit blah, a beige number. Aunt Eva favored purple. And sparkles.

"Aunt Eva once told me she would *never* marry Ted," the cousin said. "She said she'd been married once to a *great* man, and she loved him so much, she always wanted to keep his name and be remembered as his wife.

Good on you, Aunt Eva Lopez Lytle. Slow, my ass.

EPILOGUE

When the COVID-19 pandemic hit, the effect on my friends, family, and several of those I talk about in this story was devastating.

My cousin, Hank, who passed away in Spring 2020 was the first person I knew who was diagnosed with the virus, but he certainly wasn't the last. He wasn't even the last person I knew who died.

Despite intense care and every precaution, in November 2020, Jim, Molly, Erik, Erik's parents and grandparents, and three of our staff members at the veterinary clinic were diagnosed with COVID.

I, somehow, escaped. I moved into our basement for an excruciating fifteen days as I attempted to monitor the health of those I loved from afar. I'd creep up the stairs and listen to Jim's ragged breathing through the closed kitchen door. I ordered flannel sheets and footie pajamas for Molly and small treats for Erik and dropped them on their porch, just so I could see them through the window.

I called my poor, patient friend Monika—another instructor at the dance studio where I teach—incessantly. Monika had been hit hard by the virus and was trying valiantly to recover, but I harangued her daily to beg her to tell me what her symptoms were at each stage.

"They're eight days in," I said, riddled with anxiety. "What were *you* feeling eight days in?"

Erik's seventy-nine-year-old grandmother, Doris, spent several nights sleeping in the emergency room of Mercy Hospital in nearby Muskegon because there were no beds available. A dear soul who'd always been kind to me, Doris had experienced much sadness in her life, and I was terrified for her. I prayed three times each day on my knees in front of the spare bed in our basement for Doris and for my beloved Jim, Molly, and Erik. My devout father prayed that way every day of his life until his poor replacement knees could no longer sink to the floor and rise up again. And though I had long ago realized I wasn't a good fit for the Catholic Church, I still respected that aspect of my father's faith: humility. Whether it was prayer or luck or otherwise good health, my family and extended family survived, and I emerged from the basement on Thanksgiving morning 2020, more thankful than I'd been in my entire life.

But on New Year's Eve, my friend, Jeff, died of complications of the virus. Jeff was the man who'd interviewed me about my adoption, the one who asked if I'd ever felt out of place or different. He called his finished podcast "When Patti Met Mary Ann Lopez" and told his listeners, "This story is compelling and well told." Jeff was a huge supporter of mine, and he is terribly missed.

In mid-summer 2021, Jim's youngest cousin, Debra, died of COVID after several weeks spent in a Las Vegas hospital. I'd known her as a darling, dark-haired little girl, and while I'd heard she fought many demons throughout her too-short life, it was how I will always remember her.

Then in August, Cheryl, my biological oldest sister, died in Florida, leaving behind a large, loving, and devastated family.

I never felt I got to know Cheryl very well, but her loss

haunts me. Actually, maybe *because* I never got to know her very well her loss haunts me. I'd seen her maybe seven or eight times since we met.

I'd had the opportunity to introduce her to Mom and Dad; she visited their home, and we ate a fancy apple pie I bought at a bakery.

"I wasn't sure what to expect, but she seems very nice," Mom told me.

Cheryl also introduced me to her foster parents and even brought her foster mother to visit me for a fun weekend during Coast Guard Festival. The festival is a celebration held each August in Grand Haven, the small city connected to the peninsula of Spring Lake by a drawbridge over the Grand River. We led them through the streets packed with people, showed them the sights, and treated them to a viewing of "The Musical Fountain," a synchronized water and light show, which is always a tourist favorite in the resort town.

"I just *loved* the Musical *Mountain*," Cheryl told me. Jim and I call it "the Musical Mountain" as well now, in her honor.

Cheryl and I had trouble finding common ground because the only thing we seemed to share was our biology. Yet every time we spoke, which was rarely, she would end the conversation with, "Love ya." I dutifully said it in return, but in truth I always resisted the emotion. Cheryl was a very nice woman, but our lives and upbringing were different.

I assume I also have a sense of survivor guilt.

I escaped. I never knew Lois while Cheryl had known her too well, bouncing back and forth between her loving and kind foster parents and our not-so-loving-and-kind biological mother. I guarded my heart against feeling love for my oldest sibling.

I wish I could tell her I am sorry.

I spoke to so many people I mention in these pages to make sure their long-ago recollections meshed well enough with mine.

They were all sweet and accommodating. My childhood neighbor crush apologized if he ever called me a moron while we were playing chicken on our bicycles, though he said it was out of character for him and I have to agree. My high school typing teacher, Buck Heiney, apologized for playing a part in stalling my journalism career because of my lousy keyboarding skills.

One person I *didn't* check in with was my sixth-grade teacher, Mr. Dumme, who I believe either orchestrated or at least condoned the sanitary napkin humiliation in his class. I found an online photo of him and checked out his background information (no felony charges), then took the initial steps in filing a Freedom of Information Act request to find out why he was fired from Morrice Elementary a year or so after I had him as a teacher. I'd heard of his dismissal when I was in junior high but don't remember if it was a classmate or my mother who told me he was gone.

Once again, it was my friend Jackie, who had once done my eyelash extensions and is now my hair stylist, who gave me an *aha* moment. She asked if I'd told my parents about the sanitary napkin incident, and if it was why he was fired.

"No," I replied. "They never knew about it."

She looked at me in disbelief. "Patti, they knew. Even if you didn't tell them, one of the other kids in the class went home and told their parents and somebody surely told them; some mother certainly called your mother."

Of course they did. And my father was still on the school board at the time. Suddenly I wanted to know if Millie and Jim—certainly among the most protective parents on the planet—played a role in the teacher's dismissal.

I began the work necessary for a FOIA but never had to file it. Someone with knowledge of the contents of his record told me not to bother.

"He was fired, but your name was not mentioned," the person said. "The paperwork simply says he was terminated for gross incompetence."

Obviously, that doesn't mean my parents didn't play a role, but there is no evidence they did.

Almost four years after attending the quinceañera, I spoke with Terri about something that had been bothering me for a while and that I wanted to ask her.

"If I would have been raised as a Lopez and had a quinceañera like your granddaughter, would *I* have been able to wear a tiara?" I asked.

"Oh sure, Prima," she said. "Absolutely."

Figures.

On a sunny and unseasonably warm April Friday in 2021, I nervously checked and rechecked my phone, making sure text alerts were on and the ringer was set as loudly as possible. Molly was in Grand Rapids at a fertility specialty clinic, and I was awaiting the results of the visit.

When she was twenty and had been dating Erik only a short time, she dealt with incredible discomfort, made an appointment with her gynecologist, and was diagnosed with a dermoid cyst on an ovary. Surgery to remove it was scheduled, but the cyst had grown so large it had completely encompassed her organs and both the ovary and fallopian tube had to be removed.

"That's okay," many people told her. "I got pregnant with only one ovary."

A few years later, a routine ultrasound showed yet another cyst on the remaining organ. Surgery to remove it would need to be done, and while it could wait a few months until after Molly and Erik got married in May 2017, there was a small risk it would again grow larger. This time, there were no more second chances.

Molly and Erik made a quick decision and hurried through the physically brutal and enormously expensive IVF process, successfully creating ten embryos just weeks before their wedding.

"It's a precaution in the very unlikely event something more were to happen to the other ovary and fallopian tube," we told people. "They will also have the ability to adopt out the embryos if they are able to conceive the old-fashioned way and possibly help other couples with infertility issues, which of course with my history is something we are always in favor of doing."

The unlikely event *did* happen, and the following September Molly lost the other ovary and fallopian tube. Erik broke the news to her gently when she woke from surgery, and as we watched our usually stoic daughter dissolve, perhaps for the first time I felt the true impact of the grief of couples who fear they may never have a child.

"That's okay. We already have ten kids just waiting on ice. They better never complain of being cold," always optimistic Erik would tell people. But behind it all was the fear the IVF might not work or it might take *years* to work. While they were still very young, we remembered how difficult and *long* the adoption journey had been for my parents.

As time went on, Molly and Erik moved out of their first small home and bought a lovely 150-year-old farmhouse. They got a second dog, worked on their careers, did some remodeling, and suffered through their bouts with COVID. By the spring of 2021, they girded themselves to try to have a baby, hoping against hope they would be successful.

When my text alert finally went off that lovely Friday afternoon in April and I saw the message was from Molly, I

peered at my phone, very carefully reading and then reread-
ing what she'd written. Then I burst into tears.

"So, did you decide if you want to be called Nana or
Grandma?" my daughter wrote.

Molly and Erik's son, James Erickson, was born at
10:57 a.m. on New Year's Eve, 2021. Just as all my friends
who are already grandparents told me would happen, we
loved him from the moment we saw him.

He has his father's chiseled chin, his mother's pert
nose, and the face of an angel. There is so much we will
want to teach him. Jim will want to take him to Michigan
State football games and instill in him love and compassion
for animals. I'm looking forward to reminding him it is
never too late to follow a dream and reading to him from
some of his mother's favorite childhood books as he drifts
off to sleep.

And one day, maybe, I'll tell him a story from a long
time ago about a very lucky little girl and the man and the
lady who worked so hard, and for so long, to make her
their own.

ACKNOWLEDGMENTS

This book would never be in your hands without several key people who pointed out things I'd long tried to ignore, made it possible to find my biological family, and told me the stories I thought I never wanted to hear.

Jackie Jordan, eyelash extension and hairstylist extraordinaire. Jackie listened to my story and pointed me toward the truth. Honestly, I never dreamed I might have been in disguise or that my parents might have known about that teacher.

My cousins **Terri Cummings** and **Pat Kubert**. Without Terri registering for Ancestry.com and inviting me to a quinceañera only weeks after we connected, and without Pat locating a small scrap of paper her mother used to keep track of family medical issues, there would be no book.

Morrice residents **Cathy** and **Mark Edington** were willing to answer every possible question—and I had hundreds—about my hometown, from hot lunch prices in the 1960s to the length of Cork Road. Their assistance was valuable and treasured, even if they spell their last name funny.

My fifth-grade teacher at Morrice Elementary School, **Candy Zann**, was a first reader, excellent provider of critique, and one of the best cheerleaders I've ever had.

Jeff Billingsley so looked forward to hearing this story. I'll read it to you if I get to heaven, dear friend, and thank you for your constant support.

My friends **Toni Shears** and **Teresa Stevens** offered listening ears and calm voices of reason at tough moments.

So many people shared their stories of growing up in Morrice, most notably **Laurie Scott Billington**. Thanks also to my dad's best buddy **Duey Russell** for confirming that thing about transporting eyes (which people will still find hard to believe) and for loving my father like his own.

I never expected **Susie Shanahan Phillips**, daughter of the judge who handled my adoption, to take my call. But she did, and she was gracious and amazing.

I'll be forever grateful to **the residents of the town of Morrice, Michigan**. Small, but proud. Decent and loving. How lucky I was to grow up in your warm embrace.

My immense gratitude goes to **Brooke Warner** and **Addison Gallegos** of She Writes Press for their kindness, thoughtfulness and always taking time to listen; my talented editors **Krissa Lagos, Lorraine Fico-White** and **Melinda Andrews**; amazing cover designer **Leah Lococo**, and interior designer, **Tabitha Lahr**; and the astonishing publicity team of **Crystal Patriarche, Tabitha Bailey**, and **Leilani Fitzpatrick** at BookSparks.

Jasmine Rogers, thank you for riding out the storms with me, literally, to get the most wonderful author photos. I could almost hear your mom's amazing laugh as we dodged the downpours.

To my 35 member **Street Gang**, you know who you are and you know I love you. Thank you for being early readers, for taking the time out of your busy lives to help me and for telling me you laughed and you cried. You're incredible humans.

To **Kristen Lidke Woodward**, the Thelma to my Louise. Your comfort and guidance through the years when I was finding my biological family was an absolute balm to my soul.

I only knew **Aunt Eva Lopez Lytle** five years, but the impact she made on my life — and this story — is undeniable.

And of course my heart — my beloved **Jim, Molly,** and **Erik.** Thank you for being there as this story unfolded and handling it with grace and ease and humor. And **James,** one day when you are old enough to read this, please know your existence on this earth gave Gigi comfort on some of her most difficult, emotional days of writing.

Finally, I offer the biggest share of my gratitude to my parents, **Jim** and **Millie Eddington.** I hope you know I was (very, very) happy with you, as well.

ABOUT THE AUTHOR

Patti Eddington is a newspaper and magazine journalist whose favorite job ever was interviewing the famous authors who came through town on book tours. She never dreamed of writing about her life because she was too busy helping build her husband's veterinary practice, caring for her animal obsessed daughter—whose favorite childhood toy was an inflatable tick—and learning to tap dance. Then fate, and a DNA test, led her to a story she felt compelled to tell. Today, the mid-century modern design enthusiast and dance fitness instructor enjoys being dragged on walks by her ridiculous three-legged dog, David, and watching the egrets and bald eagles from her deck on a beautiful bayou in Spring Lake, Michigan.

Author photo © Jasmine Rogers

SELECTED TITLES FROM SHE WRITES PRESS

She Writes Press is an independent publishing company founded to serve women writers everywhere. Visit us at www.shewritespress.com.

Twice a Daughter: A Search for Identity, Family, and Belonging by Julie McGue. $16.95, 978-1-64742-050-5. When adopted twin Julie faces several serious health issues at age forty-eight, she sets out to find her birth parents and finally gets the family medical history she's lacking—and she ends up on a years-long quest that ultimately reveals much more than she bargained for.

All the Sweeter: Families Share Their Stories of Adopting from Foster Care by Jean Minton. $16.95, 978-1-63152-495-0. The stories of twelve families who have adopted one or more children from the US foster care system, accompanied by topical chapters that explore the common challenges these families face, including the complications that accompany transracial adoptions, helping children understand adoption, relationships with birth parents, and raising a traumatized child.

Emma's Laugh: The Gift of Second Chances by Diana Kupershmit. $16.95, 978-1-64742-112-0. After Diana's first child, Emma, is born with a rare genetic disorder, Diana relinquishes her to an adoptive family, convinced they will parent and love Emma better than she ever could—but when fate intervenes and the adoption is reversed, bringing Emma back home, Diana experiences the healing and redemptive power of love.

Fixing the Fates: An Adoptee's Story of Truth and Lies by Diane Dewey. $16.95, 978-1-63152-577-3. Since being surrendered in a German orphanage forty-seven years ago, Diane Dewey has lived with her adoptive parents near Philadelphia—loved, but deprived of information about her roots. When her Swiss biological father locates her, their reunion becomes an obsession—and ultimately leads her to the answers, and peace, she's been seeking.

Sophia's Return: Uncovering My Mother's Past by Sophia Kouidou-Giles. $16.95, 978-1-64742-171-7. Seven-year-old Sophia watches her mother leave their family home without a good-bye or explanation—a mysterious departure that becomes her worry stone. Decades later, when she returns to Greece from her adopted home in America, she uncovers a family story she had never been told.